Thank you for picking up my book. Your support means a lot, and I hope you find the read both enjoyable and insightful. Beyond being an author, my work extends into research and consultancy within organizational behavior and leadership. I engage with a broad spectrum of clients, from individuals to larger teams and organizations, offering guidance in leadership development.

For a deeper dive into my professional background and consulting philosophy, several websites are available. There, you'll also find my contact details. I'm eager to hear your thoughts on the book or discuss potential collaboration in leadership coaching.

Discover more about my work and other publications related to leadership and organizational behavior at my personal website, https://thomaspatrickhuber.com.

Learn about my specific approach to leadership coaching and consulting at https://elevateus.ch, the official website of my company.

Lastly, in case you want to reach out to me directly please send me an email at thomaspatrick@mac.com.

I appreciate your support in purchasing this book and look forward to connecting with you.

Wishing you an enlightening journey,

Thomas P Huber, PhD, MS ECS

# Dedication

To all those navigating the waves of change brought about by generative AI.

This book is dedicated to you — the leaders, the employees, the innovators, and the dreamers. To those who find themselves at the crossroads of a rapidly evolving workplace, grappling with the profound impact of generative AI. To those who are reimagining the norms, reshaping the culture, and redefining what it means to work in an era of unprecedented technological advancement.

Your resilience, adaptability, and willingness to embrace the unknown are the driving forces behind the transformation of our work environments. May this book offer guidance, insight, and encouragement as you forge new paths in creating inclusive, dynamic, and forward-thinking workplaces.

Your journey is shaping the future of work, and it is with deep respect and admiration that we dedicate this exploration to you.

# Introduction

In the opening pages of "The Future of Work Now," we set the stage for a profound exploration into two of the most defining elements reshaping today's workplace: generative AI and hybrid work models. This book is anchored in the central theme of understanding how these revolutionary forces are not only impacting the current landscape of work but are also carving out the contours of our professional future.

Generative AI, a groundbreaking facet of modern technology, is altering the very fabric of workplace operations and interactions. Its influence extends far beyond automating routine tasks, seeping into strategic decision-making, creative processes, and reshaping the skill sets required in the contemporary workforce. Meanwhile, the concept of hybrid work models – a blend of remote and in-office work – has emerged from the realms of necessity and experimentation to become a cornerstone of modern organizational strategies. This shift, accelerated by global circumstances, is not just a temporary adaptation but a redefinition of the traditional workplace.

The rationale behind delving into these topics is clear: we stand at a pivotal moment in the history of work. The convergence of advanced AI technologies with evolving work practices represents a significant leap forward, one that carries immense potential along with complex challenges. Through this book, we aim to dissect these elements, offering a comprehensive look at their implications, opportunities, and challenges.

Our exploration is not just academic; it is a practical guide for navigating this new terrain. As we investigate deeper, we invite readers to join us in uncovering the layers of this transformation, understanding its nuances, and preparing for its impact. This journey is crucial for anyone who is part of the workforce today, or plans to be in the future, as it shapes an understanding of how we can adapt, thrive, and harness the potential of these monumental shifts in the world of work.

In the ever-evolving tapestry of the modern workplace, generative AI emerges as a transformative force. This section of the introduction briefly touches upon the concept of generative AI, a type of artificial intelligence that goes beyond data analysis to actually generate new content, ideas, and solutions. Its growing influence is being felt across various sectors, fundamentally altering how businesses operate, innovate, and compete.

Generative AI is not just a technological advancement; it represents a paradigm shift in the capabilities of machines. In fields ranging from marketing and design to research and development, this technology is enabling a level of creativity and efficiency previously unattainable. Its applications are diverse – from creating realistic images and text to proposing complex problem-solving strategies and generating predictive models.

The significance of understanding AI's role in the modern workplace cannot be overstated. As we stand on the cusp of this AI revolution, it is crucial to comprehend not only its potential but also the challenges it brings. For businesses and professionals, an understanding of generative AI is becoming indispensable for staying relevant and competitive. This technology is redefining job roles, reshaping skill requirements, and setting new benchmarks for innovation and productivity.

In this context, our aim is to demystify generative AI and explore its profound impact on the workplace. It's about preparing for a future where AI is an integral part of the work environment, shaping the way we think about and approach our jobs.

Alongside the rise of generative AI, another significant transformation in the workplace has been the shift towards hybrid work models. This section of the introduction investigates how these models have emerged as a pivotal response to the changing dynamics of work. Hybrid work, a blend of remote and in-office arrangements, is redefining where and how work gets done, representing a significant evolution from traditional office-centric models.

The relevance of hybrid work models in today's work environment is multifaceted. Initially accelerated by global events like the COVID-19 pandemic, the shift to hybrid models has been further propelled by evolving employee expectations and technological advancements. Workers are increasingly seeking flexibility in their jobs, valuing the ability to balance their professional and personal lives more harmoniously. At the same time, advancements in communication and collaboration technologies have made it feasible and often more efficient to work remotely.

Exploring hybrid work models is essential because they are not merely a temporary adaptation but are becoming a permanent fixture in the work landscape. These models represent a new way of thinking about workspaces, work times, and work processes. They offer the potential for greater work-life balance, access to a broader talent pool, and cost savings for employers, but also come with challenges such as maintaining team cohesion, company culture, and ensuring equitable treatment for all employees, regardless of their physical work location.

We examine the intricacies of these hybrid work models. Understanding them is key for organizations and individuals aiming to navigate this new normal successfully. This exploration is not just about recognizing the benefits and challenges but also about equipping readers with strategies and insights to make the most of this shift.

At the heart of our exploration is a critical intersection: the integration of generative AI within hybrid work settings. This juncture represents a confluence of two major trends that are shaping the future of the workplace. The book examines how the incorporation of AI technologies in hybrid models is not just transforming the physical and digital spaces where we work but also redefining the interactions, processes, and outcomes within these environments.

Understanding the interplay between AI and hybrid work is essential in today's rapidly evolving work landscape. AI's capabilities, from automating routine tasks to providing sophisticated analytics and enhancing creative processes, offer a plethora of tools that can significantly enhance the efficiency and effectiveness of hybrid work models. These technologies enable seamless collaboration across distributed teams, ensure continuity of operations regardless of location, and open up new possibilities for innovation and problem-solving.

However, this integration also brings forth complex dynamics. It requires a careful balance between leveraging technology for productivity gains and maintaining the human touch that fosters creativity, innovation, and workplace satisfaction. The book aims to shed light on these nuances, offering insights into how organizations can harness the power of AI in a hybrid setting while nurturing a work culture that values human interaction, inclusivity, and ethical considerations.

Through this exploration, this book seeks to provide readers with a comprehensive understanding of how AI and hybrid work models are interwoven. It offers a roadmap for navigating this intersection, highlighting the strategies, challenges, and opportunities that come with adopting AI in hybrid work environments. This understanding is crucial for leaders, managers, and employees aiming to make informed decisions and adapt effectively to the changing nature of work.

Our work is a guide designed to navigate the intricate and evolving landscape of the modern workplace. This section of the introduction outlines the book's core objectives, highlighting its role as a comprehensive resource for understanding and adapting to the changes brought about by generative AI and hybrid work models.

The primary objective is to provide deep insights into how generative AI and hybrid work models are reshaping the professional world. By delving into these topics, the book aims to demystify the complexities and nuances associated with these emerging trends. It offers a thorough examination of the potential impacts, benefits, and challenges posed by the integration of AI in various work settings and the shift towards more flexible work arrangements.

The book serves as a practical guide, offering readers strategies and guidance to navigate these changes effectively. It addresses the challenges that organizations, leaders, and employees may face in this new era of work and provides solutions and best practices to overcome them. From implementing AI technologies ethically and effectively to managing and thriving in hybrid work environments, the book covers a range of essential topics.

Emphasizing its role as a guide, we equip readers with the tools and knowledge needed to adapt and succeed. Whether it's for business leaders looking to integrate AI into their operations, professionals seeking to thrive in hybrid work settings, or organizations striving to maintain a productive and engaged workforce, "The Future of Work Now" offers valuable guidance and insights.

The purpose and aim are to empower you, the reader, to embrace and navigate the changes characterizing the future of work. By providing comprehensive insights and practical guidance, the book aims to be an indispensable resource for anyone looking to understand and adapt to the evolving dynamics of the workplace in the era of AI and hybrid work models.

The book is structured into three distinct parts, each delving into key aspects of the modern work landscape shaped by generative AI and hybrid work models. This section of the introduction provides a brief overview of these parts, giving readers a glimpse into the thematic focuses and the critical topics they cover.

Part 1: Generative AI and Workplace Culture

This section embarks on an exploration of generative AI, illuminating its role in transforming workplace culture. Here, we dissect the concept of generative AI, trace its evolution, and discuss its various applications across different industries. The chapters investigate the profound impacts of AI on job roles and skills, highlighting the shift in workplace dynamics this technology brings. We also navigate through the ethical landscape surrounding AI in the workplace, addressing challenges such as bias and the balance between human intuition and automated decision-making.

Part 2: Navigating Hybrid Workplace Models

The focus shifts to the concept of hybrid work models in the second part. This segment examines the rise of these models as a response to changing work dynamics, analyzing their benefits and challenges. Key topics include the essential technologies and infrastructure that underpin effective hybrid work environments, strategies for managing remote teams, and the nuances of leading and engaging employees in a hybrid setting. Through various case studies, this part offers practical insights into implementing and thriving in hybrid work models.

Part 3: Integrating Generative AI and Hybrid Work Models

In the final part, we converge the themes of generative AI and hybrid work models, exploring how these two forces can be integrated to create more dynamic and efficient work environments. This section discusses blending AI with hybrid work cultures, upskilling for an AI-driven hybrid workplace, and managing the unique ethical considerations at this intersection. It culminates with case studies of organizations that have successfully merged AI with hybrid work models, providing readers with actionable insights and best practices.

Each part of the book is designed to offer a comprehensive understanding of its theme, equipped with real-world examples, case studies, and practical advice. The structure is thus crafted to guide readers through the complexities of these emerging trends, providing them with the knowledge and tools needed to navigate and succeed in the evolving landscape of work.

"The Future of Work Now" is crafted for a diverse audience, each playing a vital role in the evolving tapestry of the modern workplace. This book is particularly valuable for business leaders and executives who are at the forefront of implementing changes in their organizations. It offers them insights into harnessing the power of generative AI and effectively integrating hybrid work models, providing a strategic edge in today's competitive landscape.

Professionals across various sectors will find this book immensely beneficial as well. Whether they are navigating the challenges of adapting to AI-enhanced roles or thriving in hybrid work environments, the book provides practical advice and foresight into future trends that can impact their careers.

Human Resources managers and organizational development professionals are another key audience. The book offers them perspectives on managing the human element of these transitions, from upskilling employees to ensuring ethical practices in AI implementation and fostering an inclusive hybrid work culture.

This book is a valuable resource for academics, students, and researchers interested in the future of work. It provides a comprehensive analysis of current trends and future predictions, making it a useful tool for academic study and research. It is an essential read for anyone curious about the rapidly changing work landscape. Whether you are a small business owner, a startup entrepreneur, a policy maker, or simply an individual keen on staying abreast with the latest in work dynamics, this book has something for you.

As we stand on the brink of transformative changes in the workplace, "The Future of Work Now" invites you, the reader, to embark on an exploratory journey into what lies ahead. This book is not just a collection of insights and predictions; it is a voyage into the heart of the evolving work landscape, guided by the dual forces of generative AI and hybrid work models.

We encourage you to approach this journey with an open mind. The shifts and developments discussed in these pages are not mere speculations but realities unfolding in real-time. As you navigate through the chapters, you'll encounter ideas and concepts that challenge traditional notions of work, pushing the boundaries of what is possible in a modern professional setting.

Embrace the changes and challenges presented in this book. Whether you're a leader looking to steer your organization through these uncharted waters, a professional seeking to adapt and thrive, or simply an individual curious about the future of work, there is much to learn and even more to ponder.

As we set sail on this journey, remember that the future of work is not a distant dream but a present evolution. The insights you gain here are tools for understanding, adapting, and shaping this new era. So, let's turn the page and step into the future of work, together.

# Part 1: Generative AI and Workplace Culture

In Part 1 of "The Future of Work Now," we explore into the intricate relationship between generative AI and workplace culture, exploring how this advanced technology is not only redefining job roles and skill requirements but also reshaping the very ethos of the modern workplace.

We begin with a deep dive into understanding generative AI. This exploration is not just about providing a definition; it's about comprehending the essence of generative AI and how it differs from traditional forms of artificial intelligence. We trace the historical development of AI in the workplace, charting its journey from basic machine learning to the sophisticated, creative capabilities of contemporary generative AI systems. This narrative is enriched with examples illustrating how generative AI is currently being utilized across various industries, offering a glimpse into its versatile applications.

Moving forward, we examine the profound impact of AI on job roles and skills. The advent of AI is not just transforming the tasks we perform but is also ushering in a new era of skill requirements and job descriptions. We delve into the nature of these changes and explore how employees and organizations can adapt to this shift. This includes a look at innovative training methods designed to equip the workforce with the skills necessary to thrive in an AI-augmented workplace.

Ethical considerations form a crucial aspect of our discussion on AI. The deployment of AI in the workplace brings forward questions of bias, decision-making, and the balance between human intuition and automated processes. We explore these ethical dilemmas and discuss the development of frameworks aimed at guiding responsible and fair use of AI in professional settings.

Finally, we bring to life the theories and concepts discussed through a series of case studies. These real-world examples showcase how various industries are integrating AI into their operations. From success stories to lessons learned, these case studies provide valuable insights into the challenges and solutions encountered in the adoption of AI.

Part 1, therefore, sets the foundation for understanding the multifaceted impact of generative AI on the workplace, paving the way for a comprehensive discussion on how these technologies are shaping current and future work cultures.

# Chapter 1. Introduction to Generative AI

Generative AI stands at the cutting edge of artificial intelligence technology, marking a significant leap from traditional AI systems. At its core, generative AI encompasses a set of algorithms and models capable of creating new, original content or data that is indistinguishable from human-generated outputs. This technology goes beyond mere analysis and interpretation of data; it actively generates novel ideas, solutions, images, text, and even sounds based on learned patterns and structures.

One of the most striking features of generative AI is its ability to innovate and produce work that pushes the boundaries of creativity and efficiency. It has applications across a spectrum of fields – from composing music and creating art to developing new pharmaceuticals and optimizing complex systems. The potential of generative AI lies in its capacity to augment human capabilities, opening up new possibilities for exploration and discovery.

Distinction Between Generative AI and Other Forms of AI

To fully appreciate the significance of generative AI, it is essential to understand how it differs from other forms of AI. Traditional AI systems, often categorized as discriminative models, are primarily designed to recognize, classify, and respond to input data. These systems excel in tasks like categorizing images, translating languages, or recommending products based on past user behaviour. They operate by making decisions based on the data they receive, but they do not create new data or content.

Generative AI, on the other hand, is characterized by its ability to produce outputs that were not explicitly programmed or contained in its training data. It uses techniques like neural networks, particularly deep learning, to understand and replicate the complex patterns and structures within its training material. Then, it uses this understanding to generate new, original content that is often remarkably similar to human-created work.

Generative AI refers to a subset of artificial intelligence technology that is designed to create new content, solutions, or data autonomously. Unlike conventional AI systems that are programmed to analyze and interpret data to make decisions or predictions, generative AI goes a step further. It uses advanced algorithms to generate outputs that can be entirely new, not merely a reconfiguration of its input data. This form of AI is primarily based on machine learning models, particularly deep learning networks, which allow it to learn from vast datasets and produce outputs that mimic or replicate the characteristics of the input data.

## Key Characteristics that Distinguish it from Traditional AI

1. Creativity and Innovation: Generative AI can produce novel content, whether it be text, images, music, or ideas, demonstrating a form of digital creativity that is a leap beyond the capabilities of traditional AI.

2. Learning and Adapting: It learns from data patterns and can adapt its output based on this learning, enabling it to generate increasingly sophisticated and accurate creations over time.

3. Autonomy: While traditional AI systems require specific instructions and parameters to function, generative AI has a higher degree of autonomy in its ability to create without explicit guidance.

4. Predictive Modeling: Generative AI can be used to predict and model complex scenarios by generating data that represents possible future outcomes, a step beyond the predictive analytics of traditional AI.

## Types of Tasks Generative AI is Designed to Perform

1. Content Creation: This includes generating realistic images, creating music, writing textual content, and even developing video game environments.

2. Data Augmentation: Generative AI can create new data points to augment existing datasets, especially useful in scenarios where data collection is challenging or limited.

3. Simulation and Modeling: It is used to simulate complex systems or environments, providing valuable insights in fields like climate science, economics, and urban planning.

4. Problem Solving: In areas such as logistics or network optimization, generative AI can propose solutions to complex problems by generating multiple scenarios and outcomes.

5. Product Design: It can assist in the design process by generating numerous design options, iterating over them to find the most optimal solutions.

As we explore generative AI in this chapter, we will research these tasks in greater detail, examining how they are being applied across various industries and sectors. This exploration will reveal the transformative potential of generative AI, showcasing its role as a pivotal technology in the current and future landscape of work and innovation.

The story of artificial intelligence (AI) in the workplace is a fascinating journey of progression from basic, rule-based algorithms to today's sophisticated generative AI. This evolution has been shaped by a series of developments and breakthroughs, each playing a pivotal role in AI's transformation.

The inception of AI in the mid-20th century was marked by exploratory research and foundational theories. These early AI systems operated on predefined rules and logic, capable of performing basic tasks such as calculations, data sorting, and simple decision-making. Their initial applications were seen in rudimentary forms of inventory management and customer service, like automated phone systems.

As AI progressed, neural networks - inspired by the human brain's structure - were conceptualized and refined, laying the groundwork for more advanced models. This gave rise to the era of machine learning, where systems could learn and improve from experience without explicit programming. The advent of big data further fueled AI development, providing vast datasets for these systems to learn from and thereby enhancing their capabilities.

The shift from rule-based AI to machine learning and deep learning marked a significant turning point. Unlike their predecessors, these newer models didn't require detailed instructions for every task. Instead, they were capable of learning from data, making them suitable for a wider range of complex applications. This transition was instrumental in expanding AI's role in the workplace, moving beyond simple tasks to more nuanced and sophisticated functions.

The development of generative AI was propelled by key technological advancements. Sophisticated algorithms such as Generative Adversarial Networks (GANs) played a crucial role. These networks, involving two neural networks working in tandem, are capable of generating new, synthetic data instances. This innovation, coupled with the exponential growth in computational power and advances in data storage and processing technologies, allowed for the handling of the large datasets necessary to train and operate generative AI systems.

This historical trajectory of AI from its rule-based origins to the advanced generative models of today has revolutionized the workplace. It has opened up new frontiers for efficiency, creativity, and innovation, reshaping how work is done and what the future of work could look like. As we dig further into the chapters of "The Future of Work Now," we will explore the current state and potential of AI in the workplace, illuminated by this rich historical context.

Generative AI, a marvel of modern technology, is underpinned by several core technologies that enable its unique capabilities. Understanding these foundational elements provides insight into how generative AI functions and its potential applications in various domains.

Neural Networks

At the heart of generative AI are neural networks, particularly deep learning neural networks, which are inspired by the structure and function of the human brain. These networks consist of layers of interconnected nodes or 'neurons' that process and transmit information. In the context of generative AI, neural networks are trained on large datasets, learning to recognize and replicate complex patterns and structures within the data. Deep learning networks, with their multiple layers, are particularly adept at processing high volumes of data, making them ideal for tasks requiring a high degree of accuracy and detail, such as image and speech recognition.

Natural Language Processing (NLP)

Natural Language Processing (NLP) is another cornerstone of generative AI, enabling machines to understand, interpret, and generate human language. By leveraging NLP, generative AI can produce human-like text, translate languages, or even create content like poems or news articles. NLP systems use a combination of linguistic rules and machine learning models to decode and mimic language patterns, making sense of the nuances and complexities of human communication.

Machine Learning Algorithms

Generative AI also relies heavily on advanced machine learning algorithms, which allow it to learn from data and make predictions or decisions. One such algorithm is the Generative Adversarial Network (GAN), which involves two neural networks – a generator and a discriminator – working against each other. The generator creates data (like an image), and the discriminator evaluates it against real data, learning to improve its generation over time. This adversarial process results in the production of highly realistic and convincing AI-generated content.

Neural networks provide the framework for learning and data processing, NLP enables the understanding and generation of human language, and machine learning algorithms like GANs drive the creation of new, realistic outputs. Together, these technologies empower generative AI to perform a range of tasks, from creating art and music to solving complex analytical problems, making it a transformative tool in the modern workplace.

Generative AI, with its expansive capabilities, is making significant inroads across various industries. Its applications range from enhancing creativity and design to revolutionizing data analysis and customer service. Let's explore how generative AI is being utilized in different sectors and the benefits and challenges it brings to each.

In the realm of creative industries, generative AI is a game-changer. It's being used to create digital art, compose music, and even write scripts. For instance, AI algorithms can generate realistic images or animations, helping designers in conceptualizing and visualizing new ideas. In media, AI is used to create personalized content, adapting to individual preferences and enhancing user engagement.

- Benefits: AI in creative industries accelerates the creative process, offers new avenues for innovation, and personalizes user experiences.

- Challenges: There's a debate around the originality and ethical implications of AI-generated content, and concerns about AI replacing human creativity.

Generative AI is transforming business and finance by offering advanced solutions for data analysis and forecasting. AI algorithms can process vast amounts of data to identify trends and make predictions, aiding in strategic decision-making. In customer service, AI-powered chatbots are providing personalized assistance, improving customer experience and operational efficiency.

- Benefits: AI enables more accurate forecasting, efficient data processing, and enhanced customer service.

- Challenges: Reliance on AI for decision-making raises questions about accuracy, bias, and loss of human judgment in critical business decisions.

In healthcare, generative AI is playing a pivotal role in diagnostics and treatment planning. AI algorithms can analyze medical images to assist in diagnosing diseases, and in treatment planning, AI can help in creating personalized medicine regimens based on patient-specific data.

- Benefits: AI contributes to more accurate diagnoses, personalized treatment plans, and the potential for breakthroughs in complex medical research.

- Challenges: There are concerns about data privacy, the need for robust datasets to train AI, and ensuring AI complements rather than replaces the physician's expertise.

Manufacturing and logistics are benefiting from AI-driven automation and predictive maintenance. AI systems can optimize production processes, manage supply chains, and predict equipment failures before they occur, thereby reducing downtime and maintenance costs.
- Benefits: Enhanced efficiency, reduced operational costs, and improved product quality are significant benefits.

- Challenges: Implementation costs, the need for continuous data input and analysis, and the potential impact on employment in traditional manufacturing roles.

In each of these industries, generative AI brings a unique set of benefits and challenges. While it offers increased efficiency, enhanced creativity, and more informed decision-making, it also presents concerns such as ethical considerations, the potential for job displacement, and the need for robust data governance. As we continue to explore the applications of AI, these benefits and challenges will shape how AI is integrated and evolved in various sectors.

Generative AI is revolutionizing the workplace by significantly optimizing efficiency and productivity. Its impact is felt in various work processes, where it not only streamlines operations but also brings a new level of creativity and insight.

In terms of efficiency, generative AI is capable of automating complex tasks that traditionally required significant human input. By processing and analyzing large sets of data at unprecedented speeds, it identifies patterns and insights that can improve operational efficiency. For instance, in sectors like retail and logistics, AI can predict consumer behavior or optimize supply chain management, leading to more efficient resource allocation and inventory management.

The role of generative AI in enhancing productivity extends beyond mere automation. It also assists in decision-making processes. In the financial sector, AI algorithms are used to analyze market trends and advise on investment strategies, thus enabling faster and more informed decisions. In marketing, AI tools can analyze consumer data to tailor marketing strategies, enhancing the effectiveness of campaigns.

Generative AI is making a significant mark in creative processes. In design and content creation, for example, AI tools are being used to generate new concepts and ideas, pushing the boundaries of creativity. These tools can propose design alternatives, write creative copy, or even compose music, providing creative professionals with a powerful tool to explore new possibilities.

This integration of AI into work processes is not without its challenges. While AI can enhance efficiency and creativity, there is an ongoing need to balance AI-driven automation with human oversight. Ensuring that AI complements human skills, rather than replacing them, is crucial for maintaining the quality and integrity of work processes.

As we contemplate the future of generative AI in the workplace, it's clear that its trajectory is poised to reshape not only how we work but also the broader contours of the global economy and societal norms. The future developments of generative AI are expected to be groundbreaking. We anticipate advancements that will make AI even more intuitive, creative, and capable of handling complex tasks that currently require human expertise. This evolution could lead to AI systems that are not just tools but collaborators in creative and strategic processes. For example, in the field of research and development, AI might play a key role in discovering new materials or drugs, dramatically speeding up the innovation cycle.

The impact of generative AI on various job sectors could be profound. In sectors like manufacturing, AI could lead to more efficient production lines and predictive maintenance, reducing downtime and costs. In services and customer relations, AI is likely to enable more personalized and efficient customer experiences. However, this also brings the challenge of job displacement in roles that become automated by AI, necessitating a focus on reskilling and upskilling employees.

The global economy could see significant shifts due to the widespread adoption of generative AI. There could be a surge in productivity and efficiency across various industries, leading to economic growth. However, this might also lead to disparities between businesses and economies that can effectively integrate AI and those that cannot, potentially widening the economic gap.

Ethical and societal implications will be at the forefront of the widespread adoption of generative AI. Questions around data privacy, security, and the ethical use of AI-generated content will become increasingly important. There will be a need for clear regulatory frameworks and ethical guidelines to ensure that the use of AI is responsible and beneficial to society as a whole. Additionally, as AI becomes more prevalent, its societal impact, particularly on employment and privacy, will require careful management and thoughtful solutions.

The future of generative AI in the workplace presents a landscape filled with potential and challenges. Its advancements promise to bring efficiency and innovation, but they also necessitate careful consideration of the ethical, societal, and economic implications. As we move forward, the focus will be on harnessing the benefits of AI while responsibly addressing its challenges, shaping a future that leverages technology for the greater good of businesses, economies, and societies.

As we conclude this chapter on the historical development and core technologies behind generative AI, we have traversed through its emergence, evolution, and the intricate technologies that constitute its foundation. We've seen how generative AI, from its early rule-based systems to the sophisticated machine learning and neural network-based models of today, represents a significant leap in the capabilities of artificial intelligence. This progression from basic data processing to the creation of new, innovative content and solutions marks a pivotal shift in the potential of AI.

We jumped into the core technologies that drive generative AI, such as neural networks that mimic the human brain, natural language processing that enables machines to interpret and generate human-like language, and advanced machine learning algorithms like GANs that facilitate the creation of entirely new data. These technologies together form the backbone of generative AI, enabling it to impact various industries by optimizing processes, enhancing creativity, and aiding in complex decision-making.

We have explored the applications of generative AI across different sectors, from the creative industries where it's pushing the boundaries of art and design, to business and finance where it's revolutionizing data analysis and customer service, to healthcare and manufacturing where it's enhancing diagnostics and predictive maintenance. Each of these applications demonstrates the transformative potential of generative AI in enhancing efficiency, creativity, and strategic insights.

It's clear that the journey of generative AI is one of constant evolution and innovation, carrying significant implications for the future of work. The technologies we have discussed lay the groundwork for a deeper exploration of how AI is reshaping the workplace. Moving forward, our next chapter will examine the impact of AI on job roles and skills. We will explore how the advancement of AI technologies is not just automating tasks but also creating new job roles and necessitating a shift in the skills required in the modern workplace. Join us as we continue to navigate the ever-evolving landscape of work in the age of AI.

# Chapter 2: AI's Impact on Job Roles and Skills

In chapter 2 of "The Future of Work Now," our focus shifts to the profound influence of artificial intelligence on the workplace. AI's presence in the professional sphere has grown exponentially, not just in terms of technological infrastructure but also in how it redefines roles and reshapes skill sets. This chapter aims to contextualize and examine the depth of AI's impact on job roles and skills.

The integration of AI into various industries has transcended the bounds of mere technological novelty; it has become a fundamental component of operational and strategic functions in organizations. From automating routine tasks to providing complex analytics and facilitating creative processes, AI's capabilities are both enhancing and transforming the nature of work. This evolution is not limited to specific sectors but is a widespread phenomenon, influencing a diverse range of professions and disciplines.

As AI continues to advance, its influence on job roles is twofold. On one hand, it automates and streamlines tasks, leading to changes in job descriptions and the possible redundancy of certain roles. On the other hand, AI opens up new avenues for innovation and creativity, leading to the emergence of new job roles that require a unique set of skills centered around AI technology.

Simultaneously, the skill requirements in the workplace are undergoing a significant shift. The rise of AI demands a workforce that is not only tech-savvy but also adaptable and continuous learners. Skills such as AI literacy, data analytics, and an understanding of machine learning are becoming increasingly important. Equally critical are the soft skills like critical thinking, problem-solving, and the ability to work collaboratively with AI systems.

We will dive deeper into these changes, exploring how AI is reshaping job roles across various industries and the emerging skills that are becoming essential for professionals. We aim to provide a comprehensive understanding of AI's transforming role in the workplace, offering insights into how individuals and organizations can adapt to and thrive in this new era of work.

AI's impact on traditional job roles is evident across a wide array of industries. In sectors like manufacturing, AI-driven automation is changing the nature of factory work, reducing the need for manual labor in certain processes and shifting the focus to more skilled tasks like machine supervision and quality control. In fields such as customer service, AI chatbots and virtual assistants are taking over routine inquiries, allowing human employees to focus on more complex customer interactions that require empathy and nuanced understanding.

The emergence of new roles specifically created due to AI integration is a fascinating development. These include positions like AI trainers, who teach AI systems how to interpret and react to human interactions, and AI ethicists, who ensure AI solutions are developed and implemented in an ethical manner. Data scientists and machine learning engineers are in high demand, tasked with creating and refining AI algorithms.

The shift in job responsibilities brought about by AI is significant. AI complements human skills, automating tasks that are repetitive and time-consuming, which allows human workers to focus on areas where they excel, such as creative problem-solving, strategic planning, and interpersonal communication. This complementary relationship between AI and human skills is leading to more collaborative work environments where AI systems and human employees work in tandem to enhance productivity and innovation.

The transformation in job roles due to AI integration is multifaceted. While it presents challenges, such as the need for reskilling and potential job displacement in certain sectors, it also opens up new opportunities for professional growth and the development of innovative work practices. As we delve further into this chapter, we will analyze these changes in greater detail, providing insights into how the workforce can adapt to and benefit from the evolving role of AI in the workplace.

As artificial intelligence becomes increasingly integrated into the workplace, it necessitates a shift in the skill sets required by professionals across various sectors. This integration is not only revolutionizing job roles but also reshaping the competencies needed for success in an AI-driven work environment.

The integration of AI in the workplace has created a growing demand for technical skills directly related to AI and data literacy. Professionals are now required to have a basic understanding of how AI systems work, including knowledge of machine learning, data analysis, and algorithmic processes. In many sectors, the ability to interpret and leverage insights from AI-generated data is becoming crucial. For instance, marketing professionals are using AI-driven data analytics to understand customer behavior, while finance professionals are leveraging AI for market analysis and risk assessment.

There's a noticeable shift towards advanced technical skills in areas such as AI programming, machine learning model development, and data engineering. These skills are becoming essential in industries heavily reliant on AI, such as tech, finance, and healthcare. The ability to not only use but also develop and manage AI systems is becoming a highly valued skill set, leading to new career opportunities and job roles.

Beyond technical skills, the importance of soft skills in an AI-driven work environment is becoming increasingly prominent. As AI takes over more routine and analytical tasks, skills like critical thinking, creativity, and problem-solving are more important than ever. These skills enable professionals to complement AI's capabilities by providing insight and decision-making that AI cannot replicate.

Interpersonal skills such as communication, collaboration, and empathy are also gaining importance. In a workplace where human employees increasingly interact with AI systems, the ability to effectively communicate and work alongside AI technology is crucial. Moreover, as AI alters job roles, professionals need to adapt, requiring a high degree of flexibility and a willingness to engage in continuous learning and development.

The integration of artificial intelligence into the workplace has instigated a fundamental shift in the landscape of professional competencies. This part of the chapter researches how these competencies are evolving in response to AI, highlighting the need for a balanced skill set that combines technical know-how with adaptive, human-centric skills.

With AI becoming a staple in many industries, technical competencies related to AI and data science are increasingly sought after. This includes skills in programming, machine learning, data analytics, and understanding AI algorithms. Such technical expertise is vital for developing, managing, and leveraging AI systems effectively. Professionals in fields ranging from IT and engineering to marketing and finance are finding it increasingly necessary to gain a foundational understanding of these technologies to stay relevant and competitive.

As much as technical skills are in demand, there's a growing recognition of the value of adaptive skills. AI, despite its advanced capabilities, cannot replicate human creativity, strategic thinking, and problem-solving. In this new work landscape, the ability to think creatively, develop innovative solutions, and solve complex problems is becoming more critical. These skills enable professionals to leverage AI as a tool for enhancing their work, rather than being overshadowed by it.

The balance between technical skills and soft skills like communication, empathy, and teamwork is more important than ever. As AI alters traditional roles and creates new ones, professionals need to collaborate effectively with both AI systems and their human colleagues. The ability to communicate complex AI concepts in an understandable manner, empathize with team members' challenges, and work collaboratively in diverse teams is vital.

The evolving landscape of professional competencies also underscores the importance of a continuous learning mindset. As AI technologies advance, staying abreast of the latest developments and adapting one's skill set becomes crucial. This includes engaging in ongoing education and training, whether through formal courses, workshops, or self-learning. As the workplace increasingly integrates artificial intelligence, the need for innovative training methods and educational initiatives to upskill employees becomes crucial. This part of the chapter focuses on various strategies and programs designed to equip the workforce with the necessary skills for an AI-integrated work environment.

Corporate training programs are at the forefront of this upskilling effort. Many organizations are developing in-house training modules focused on AI and digital literacy. These programs are tailored to the specific needs of the business and often include hands-on learning experiences. They cover a range of topics from basic AI concepts and data literacy to more advanced subjects like machine learning and AI application in specific business functions.

Online courses and workshops offer another avenue for skill development. There is a plethora of online platforms providing courses in AI, data science, and related fields. These courses range from introductory to advanced levels, making them accessible to employees with varying degrees of prior knowledge. Workshops, often more interactive and targeted, provide opportunities for employees to apply their learning in practical scenarios and problem-solving exercises.

Partnerships between educational institutions and businesses are playing a pivotal role in preparing the future workforce. These collaborations often involve co-developing curriculum that incorporates AI and data literacy, ensuring that the education provided is relevant and applicable to the current job market. Internship and co-op programs, part of these partnerships, offer students real-world experience in AI-integrated work settings, bridging the gap between academic learning and professional requirements.

Mentorship programs within organizations can facilitate knowledge transfer from more experienced employees who have a robust understanding of AI applications in business contexts. This peer-to-peer learning approach can be particularly effective in contextualizing AI skills within specific job roles. A combination of corporate training programs, online education, workshops, and partnerships with educational institutions forms a comprehensive approach to upskilling employees for an AI-integrated workplace. As we further explore this topic, the chapter will highlight the importance of continuous learning and adaptability, providing insights into how organizations and individuals can navigate the evolving landscape of professional competencies in the age of AI.

The rapidly evolving landscape of artificial intelligence necessitates a paradigm shift in how both individuals and organizations approach skill development. Continuous learning and adaptability are no longer optional but essential for success in this AI-augmented era. This part of the chapter discusses the imperative of fostering a culture of lifelong learning and the strategies organizations can implement to cultivate this mindset.

In an AI-driven work environment, technologies and best practices are in a constant state of flux. This dynamic nature of AI means that the skills and knowledge that are relevant today may evolve or become obsolete tomorrow. For professionals, this environment demands a commitment to continuous learning – an ongoing process of developing new skills and knowledge to stay abreast of technological advancements. For organizations, it involves creating an ecosystem that not only encourages but also enables this continual growth and adaptation.

One effective strategy for organizations is to integrate learning into the fabric of their workplace culture. This can be achieved by offering regular training sessions, workshops, and seminars that focus on emerging AI technologies and their applications in the industry. Encouraging participation in these programs can be further incentivized through recognition, rewards, or incorporating them into career development plans. Creating opportunities for experiential learning is another key strategy. This can include hands-on projects involving AI applications, hackathons, or collaboration with tech firms on real-world problems. Such experiences allow employees to apply their theoretical knowledge in practical settings, enhancing their understanding and skills.

Organizations can invest in digital learning platforms that offer a range of courses and resources on AI and related fields. These platforms should be accessible and flexible, allowing employees to learn at their own pace and according to their personal and professional commitments.

Mentorship programs within the organization can also play a significant role. Pairing less experienced employees with AI-savvy mentors creates opportunities for knowledge transfer and practical guidance, fostering a learning community within the workplace. Leadership plays a crucial role in fostering a learning culture. Leaders who prioritize their own continuous learning set a powerful example for their teams. They can also advocate for and implement policies that support education, skill development, and innovation.

As the AI landscape continues to evolve rapidly, the need for continuous learning and adaptability becomes increasingly critical. For individuals, it means a commitment to lifelong education. For organizations, it involves creating an environment that supports and encourages this ongoing development. By embracing these strategies, both can navigate the challenges and opportunities presented by AI, ensuring readiness and relevance in the future of work.

In exploring the skill transformation necessitated by the integration of artificial intelligence in the workplace, real-world examples offer valuable insights. These case examples showcase organizations that have successfully navigated the shift in skills due to AI, providing lessons learned and best practices that can be applied broadly.

One notable example is a global technology company that undertook a comprehensive AI training program for its employees. Recognizing the shift towards AI-driven processes, the company launched an initiative to upskill its workforce, offering a mix of in-house training sessions, online courses, and collaborative learning opportunities. This approach not only enhanced the employees' technical skills in AI but also fostered a culture of continuous learning within the organization.

Another case involves a financial services firm that integrated AI into its operations for better data analysis and customer service. To adapt to this change, the firm implemented a structured training program focused on data literacy and AI applications in finance. The program was designed to be inclusive, catering to employees with varying levels of technical expertise. The firm also encouraged a collaborative learning environment where employees could share insights and applications of AI in their work, leading to a more cohesive and AI-literate workforce.

A healthcare organization provides another compelling example. With the introduction of AI for patient data analysis and diagnostic procedures, the organization faced the challenge of aligning its staff with these new technologies. It responded by partnering with educational institutions to develop tailored training programs for its healthcare professionals. These programs combined theoretical knowledge of AI with practical applications in healthcare, ensuring that the staff could effectively integrate AI into their practice.

From these case examples, several lessons and best practices emerge:

1.  Tailored Training Programs: Successful skill transformation initiatives are often those that are tailored to the specific needs of the organization and its employees.

2.  Inclusivity and Accessibility: Ensuring that training and upskilling programs are accessible to employees at all levels of technical proficiency encourages widespread adoption and integration of AI.

3.  Collaborative Learning Environments: Fostering a culture where employees can share knowledge and insights about AI applications enhances learning and encourages innovation.

4.  Leadership Commitment: Active support and involvement from leadership are crucial in driving the success of skill transformation initiatives.

5.  Partnerships with Educational Institutions: Collaborating with universities or training providers can bring valuable expertise and resources to an organization's training programs.

These case examples demonstrate that with thoughtful strategies and commitment, organizations can effectively navigate the skill shift brought about by AI. By learning from these examples, other organizations can develop their own approaches to skill transformation, ensuring their workforce is equipped to thrive in an AI-integrated workplace.

This chapter has highlighted the significant shift in professional competencies necessitated by the rise of artificial intelligence. We observed how traditional job roles are evolving, with AI automating routine tasks and creating new opportunities for human creativity and strategic thinking. The emergence of entirely new job roles, specifically tailored to AI integration, marks a significant shift in the professional landscape.

We probed the growing demand for a dual skill set, where technical proficiency in AI and data literacy is as important as adaptive skills like problem-solving and critical thinking. The chapter also explored innovative strategies for upskilling and reskilling employees, emphasizing the need for continuous learning in an AI-driven work environment. Through real-world examples, we gleaned valuable lessons and best practices that organizations have implemented to successfully navigate this skill shift.

As we transition to the next chapter, the focus will shift from the transformation of job roles and skills to the ethical considerations surrounding the integration of AI in the workplace. This next chapter will address the crucial questions of ethical AI use, including the challenges of data privacy, potential biases in AI algorithms, and the balance between technological advancement and ethical responsibility. We will explore how organizations can develop ethical frameworks and strategies to ensure that AI is used in a way that is not only efficient and innovative but also responsible and aligned with societal values. The upcoming chapter aims to provide a comprehensive understanding of the ethical dimensions of AI in the workplace, a topic that is becoming increasingly important as AI becomes more ingrained in our professional and personal lives.

# Chapter 3: Ethical Considerations in AI

We now turn our attention to exploring the complex and increasingly critical realm of ethical considerations in artificial intelligence. This chapter opens by painting a broad overview of the ethical landscape that has emerged alongside the rapid advancements in AI technology. The intersection of AI with various aspects of professional and personal life has brought to the forefront a range of ethical dilemmas and considerations that demand our attention and careful analysis.

The ethical challenges in AI are as diverse as the applications of the technology itself. They span issues of privacy, bias, accountability, transparency, and the broader impact of AI on society and human well-being. As AI systems become more capable and are entrusted with more significant decisions and tasks, the ethical implications of their development and application become more pronounced and complex.

Recognizing the importance of ethics in AI is crucial, not only for the sustainable and responsible development of the technology but also for maintaining public trust and social license to operate. Ethical AI development and application involve ensuring that AI systems do not inadvertently perpetuate biases, invade privacy, or make unaccountable decisions with far-reaching consequences. It also involves considering the broader societal implications, such as the potential impact on employment, equity, and social dynamics.

This chapter sets out to explore these ethical considerations in depth, examining the challenges they pose, and the strategies being developed to address them. By establishing a clear understanding of the ethical landscape in AI, we lay the groundwork for a discussion that is increasingly relevant and necessary in a world where AI is becoming an integral part of the fabric of our work and lives.

AI bias refers to the tendency of AI systems to produce results that are systematically prejudiced due to erroneous assumptions in the machine learning process. This bias can manifest in various forms, including data bias, algorithmic bias, and societal bias. Data bias occurs when the datasets used to train AI algorithms are not representative of the broader population or reality, leading to skewed results. Algorithmic bias arises from the way algorithms are designed and the inherent prejudices they may contain. Societal bias reflects existing societal prejudices and stereotypes that can be inadvertently encoded into AI systems.

The introduction of biases into AI algorithms often stems from the data used to train these systems. Since AI algorithms learn to make decisions based on the data they are fed, any inherent biases in the data will likely be reflected in the AI's behavior. For instance, if an AI system is trained on historical hiring data that contains gender bias, it may replicate these biases in its screening of job applicants.

The implications of AI bias are far-reaching and can have significant impacts in sectors such as employment, finance, and criminal justice. In employment, AI bias can lead to unfair job screening processes, where candidates are assessed based on biased criteria. In finance, AI systems used for credit scoring or loan approvals may exhibit biases against certain demographic groups. In criminal justice, AI tools used for predictive policing or sentencing risk assessments may perpetuate racial biases, affecting the fairness of legal processes.

A notable case study illustrating the real-world impact of AI bias involved an AI recruiting tool used by a tech company. The tool was found to be biased against female candidates, as it was trained on resumes submitted over a decade, most of which were from men. This led to the AI system favoring male candidates over equally or more qualified female candidates. The company had to abandon the tool and reassess its approach to AI in hiring processes.

This case study, among others, underscores the crucial need for vigilance, continuous monitoring, and corrective measures to mitigate AI bias. Addressing AI bias requires a multifaceted approach, including diversifying training data, designing algorithms with fairness in mind, and implementing oversight mechanisms to monitor and correct biased outcomes. As AI continues to permeate various aspects of our lives, the ethical imperative to tackle AI bias head-on becomes increasingly important, ensuring that AI systems are fair, equitable, and just.

The challenge of AI bias is not insurmountable. There are effective strategies and approaches that can be employed to identify and reduce bias in AI systems. This section of the chapter explores these strategies, emphasizing the importance of data diversity, algorithmic transparency, and ethical data collection and processing.

Strategies for Identifying and Reducing Bias in AI Systems

The first step in addressing AI bias is its identification. This involves a thorough analysis of AI systems to detect any skewed results or discriminatory patterns. One effective approach is to conduct regular audits of AI algorithms and the outcomes they produce, looking for discrepancies that may indicate bias. Another strategy is to implement 'bias testing' protocols as part of the AI development process, where AI systems are intentionally exposed to various scenarios to check for biased responses.

Once bias is identified, steps can be taken to mitigate it. One method is to refine or retrain AI algorithms with more diverse and representative datasets. This helps in reducing data bias, ensuring that the AI system's learning is based on a broad and inclusive range of data inputs. In some cases, it may be necessary to redesign the algorithm itself, especially if the bias is deeply ingrained in the way the algorithm processes data.

Role of Data Diversity and Algorithmic Transparency

Data diversity plays a crucial role in combating AI bias. Diverse datasets that accurately reflect the diversity of the real world can help in training AI systems that are fair and unbiased. This involves not only including data from diverse demographics but also ensuring a variety of viewpoints and scenarios are represented.

Algorithmic transparency is another key factor. Making AI algorithms transparent and understandable helps in identifying potential sources of bias. It involves clearly documenting how algorithms are designed, how they make decisions, and the nature of the data they are trained on. This transparency is crucial for both developers and end-users, as it allows for greater scrutiny and understanding of AI decision-making processes.

Ethical Considerations in Data Collection and Processing

Ethical data collection and processing are paramount in ensuring AI fairness. This means obtaining data through fair and legal means, respecting privacy rights, and ensuring consent where necessary. It also involves being mindful of the potential for data to reflect existing societal biases and taking steps to account for and counteract these biases.

The ethical processing of data also includes being vigilant about the ways in which data is used to train AI. This means not only using data that is representative and diverse but also being aware of the context in which data is gathered and used, ensuring that it does not perpetuate harmful stereotypes or inequalities.

Addressing and mitigating AI bias is a multifaceted endeavor that requires careful attention to the ways in which AI systems are developed, trained, and deployed. By employing strategies such as regular audits, bias testing, data diversity, algorithmic transparency, and ethical data practices, it is possible to reduce the impact of bias in AI systems. As we move forward, these strategies will be crucial in ensuring that AI technologies are used in a manner that is fair, just, and equitable.

In the evolving landscape of artificial intelligence, the interaction between AI decision-making and human intuition presents a fascinating dynamic. This section of the chapter delves into the complexities of integrating AI into decision-making processes, the balance of benefits and challenges this integration brings, and the crucial role of human oversight in AI-driven environments.

## The Dynamic Between AI Decision-Making and Human Intuition

The collaboration between AI and humans in decision-making processes is characterized by a blend of computational efficiency and human insight. AI systems excel in handling large datasets, identifying patterns, and making predictions based on statistical probabilities. However, they often lack the nuanced understanding and emotional intelligence inherent to human intuition. Human decision-makers, on the other hand, can interpret context, understand subtleties, and apply ethical and moral reasoning that AI systems cannot. This synergy of AI's analytical prowess and human intuition can lead to more informed, balanced, and comprehensive decision-making.

## Benefits and Challenges of AI Integration in Decision-Making

Integrating AI into decision-making processes offers numerous benefits. It can enhance efficiency, reduce the likelihood of human error, and provide data-driven insights that might be difficult for humans to discern unaided. In sectors like healthcare, AI can assist in diagnosing diseases by analyzing medical images with precision. In business, AI-driven analytics can inform strategic decisions by providing a comprehensive view of market trends.

This integration is not without challenges. Over-reliance on AI can lead to complacency, where the human role in decision-making is undervalued. There's also the risk of algorithmic opacity, where decision-makers don't fully understand how the AI reached its conclusions, making it difficult to evaluate the reliability of its recommendations. Additionally, AI systems can sometimes make errors or operate with biases, as discussed in the previous sections.

The Role of Human Oversight in AI-Driven Environments

Human oversight in AI-driven environments is crucial to ensure that AI systems function as intended and ethical standards are maintained. It involves humans monitoring AI decisions, understanding the rationale behind these decisions, and intervening when necessary. This oversight ensures that AI systems remain aligned with organizational goals and ethical norms.

Incorporating human oversight also means setting up checks and balances where AI recommendations are critically evaluated and not accepted blindly. This could involve a multidisciplinary approach, where experts from different fields collaborate to interpret AI findings and apply them appropriately.

The collaboration between AI and human decision-making is a delicate balance that needs to be carefully managed. While AI can significantly enhance decision-making processes, human oversight and intuition are indispensable to ensure that these processes remain effective, ethical, and aligned with broader human values. As we progress, understanding and managing this collaboration will be key to harnessing the full potential of AI in various domains.

As we probe the ethical aspects of AI in the workplace, developing and adhering to robust ethical frameworks becomes paramount. This section of the chapter discusses the creation of guidelines for ethical AI use, examines existing frameworks and standards, and explores the role of governance and regulatory bodies in shaping these ethics.

Developing Guidelines for Ethical AI Use in the Workplace
Creating guidelines for ethical AI use involves establishing clear principles that govern how AI is developed, deployed, and utilized in the workplace. These guidelines typically encompass issues

such as fairness, transparency, accountability, and privacy. They serve as a foundation for ensuring AI is used in a way that is not only efficient and effective but also ethical and responsible.

For instance, fairness in AI involves ensuring that AI systems do not perpetuate or amplify biases. Transparency relates to how AI decisions are made and the ability to explain these decisions in understandable terms. Accountability addresses who is responsible for AI's decisions, particularly in cases where these decisions have significant consequences. Privacy considerations include how data used by AI is collected, stored, and processed.

Discussing Existing Ethical Frameworks and Standards for AI

There are several existing ethical frameworks and standards for AI that organizations can look to when developing their own guidelines. These include the Ethics Guidelines for Trustworthy AI by the European Commission, which outlines seven key requirements for trustworthy AI, including human oversight and technical robustness. Similarly, the IEEE Global Initiative on Ethics of Autonomous and Intelligent Systems offers comprehensive standards and recommendations for ethically aligned AI design.

These frameworks provide valuable insights and serve as a reference point for organizations looking to navigate the ethical dimensions of AI use. They highlight common concerns and best practices, offering a starting point for crafting tailored ethical guidelines.

The Role of Governance and Regulatory Bodies in Shaping AI Ethics

Governance and regulatory bodies play a crucial role in shaping the ethical landscape of AI. These bodies set the legal and regulatory frameworks within which AI operates, ensuring that there are standards and accountability mechanisms in place. Their role involves not just enforcing compliance but also guiding the development of AI in a direction that aligns with societal values and norms.

Regulatory bodies can also drive the conversation on AI ethics by bringing together stakeholders from various sectors to discuss and address ethical challenges. This collaboration can lead to the development of more comprehensive and practical guidelines that are adaptable to the changing nature of AI technologies.

Developing ethical frameworks for AI use is a critical step in ensuring that AI benefits are maximized while minimizing potential harms. By drawing on existing frameworks and standards and engaging with governance and regulatory bodies, organizations can create a solid foundation for ethical AI use. As we continue to explore the multifaceted aspects of AI in the workplace, these ethical considerations will remain a central theme, guiding how AI is integrated and utilized in professional settings.

Fostering an ethical AI culture within organizations is a multifaceted endeavor that extends beyond the establishment of guidelines and policies. It involves ingraining ethical awareness and practices into the very fabric of the organizational culture. One effective strategy to achieve this is through comprehensive training and awareness programs for employees focused on AI ethics. These programs should aim to educate employees about the importance of ethical considerations in AI, including fairness, transparency, privacy, and accountability. They can be structured as workshops, seminars, or e-learning courses that cover real-world scenarios and ethical dilemmas that might arise in AI usage.

In addition to formal training programs, creating an environment that encourages open dialogue about AI ethics is crucial. This can be facilitated through regular meetings, forums, or discussions where employees can share their experiences, concerns, and insights about AI applications. Such platforms not only enhance understanding but also foster a culture of collective responsibility and proactive ethical behavior in AI usage.

Leadership plays a vital role in cultivating an ethical AI culture. Leaders must lead by example, demonstrating a commitment to ethical AI practices in their decision-making and operations. They can also champion initiatives that promote ethical AI use and ensure that ethical considerations are a key part of AI-related projects and strategies.

Fostering an ethical AI culture requires a proactive and comprehensive approach that involves educating employees, encouraging open discussions, and setting the tone at the leadership level. This culture is fundamental to ensuring that AI is used responsibly and beneficially within organizations.

As we look toward the future of artificial intelligence, it's imperative to prepare for the ethical challenges that lie ahead in the ever-evolving AI landscape. Anticipating these future dilemmas requires a proactive approach, one that acknowledges the rapid pace at which AI technologies and their applications are developing. Ethical challenges that may arise in the future could stem from advancements in AI capabilities, such as increased autonomy in decision-making processes or the integration of AI in more personal aspects of human life.

The importance of continuous ethical evaluation and adaptation in AI practices cannot be overstated. As AI systems become more complex and ingrained in various sectors, the ethical considerations surrounding them will also become more intricate. It's crucial for organizations to not only establish initial ethical guidelines but to also commit to ongoing evaluation and updating of these standards. This dynamic approach ensures that ethical practices keep pace with technological advancements and changing societal norms.

This continuous ethical vigilance involves regularly reviewing and updating AI policies, staying informed about the latest developments in AI technology and ethics, and maintaining an open dialogue with stakeholders about ethical concerns. It also includes actively monitoring AI systems for unintended biases or consequences and being ready to modify these systems as needed.

Organizations should foster a culture of ethical awareness, where employees are encouraged to think critically about the implications of their work with AI and feel empowered to raise ethical concerns. This culture can be supported through ongoing education and training, as well as by leadership that prioritizes ethical considerations in all AI-related initiatives.

Preparing for future ethical challenges in AI is a dynamic and continuous process. It requires organizations to remain agile and responsive, ensuring that their use of AI is not only technologically advanced but also ethically sound and aligned with broader societal values. This proactive stance is key to navigating the complex ethical terrain of the future AI landscape.

As we conclude the discussion on AI ethics, we have traversed a landscape rich with complex challenges and considerations. This chapter has illuminated the multifaceted nature of ethical issues in AI, from the inherent biases in algorithms to the dynamic interplay between AI decision-making and human intuition. We explored the strategies for addressing and mitigating AI bias, the importance of fostering an ethical AI culture within organizations, and the necessity of preparing for future ethical challenges.

The ethical considerations of AI are not just theoretical concerns but are deeply entwined with the practicalities of how AI is developed, implemented, and managed in real-world settings. As AI continues to permeate various aspects of our professional and personal lives, the importance of ethical vigilance cannot be overstated. It is a responsibility that extends beyond technologists and data scientists to include all stakeholders in the AI ecosystem.

Next, we will shift our focus from the theoretical and ethical aspects to real-world applications and implications. The upcoming chapter delves into case studies of AI integration across different industries. These stories will provide tangible examples of how AI is being applied, the challenges encountered, and the innovative solutions developed. Through these case studies, we will gain insights into the practical aspects of AI integration, learning from the successes and setbacks experienced by organizations on the front lines of AI adoption. This exploration aims to provide a comprehensive view of AI in action, offering valuable lessons and best practices that can guide organizations in their AI journey.

# Chapter 4: Case Studies in AI Integration

Are you ready to jump into the practical side of AI integration, exploring its widespread adoption across various industries? This chapter aims to bring to life the concepts and ethical considerations discussed earlier through real-world applications and experiences. The landscape of AI integration is vast and varied, touching nearly every sector in some form, from healthcare and finance to manufacturing and retail.

We set the stage for a deep dive into a diverse range of industry-specific AI applications. Each sector presents its unique challenges and opportunities for AI integration, shaping the tools and technologies used. In healthcare, for instance, AI is revolutionizing patient care and medical research, while in finance, it's reshaping how we approach everything from investment strategies to fraud detection. Manufacturing sees AI optimizing production processes, and in the world of retail, AI is transforming the customer experience.

These industry-specific applications of AI are not just transforming operational processes but are also reshaping the workforce and raising new ethical considerations. As we explore these case studies, we gain insights into how organizations navigate the complexities of AI implementation – from the initial stages of integration to addressing challenges like workforce training and ethical dilemmas.

The case studies in this chapter are carefully selected to provide a comprehensive understanding of the practical realities of AI integration. They offer a glimpse into the successes achieved and the lessons learned, providing valuable guidance for organizations embarking on their own AI journeys. By examining these real-world examples, the chapter aims to bridge the gap between theory and practice, offering readers a vivid picture of AI's potential and its impact on the future of work.

As we go deeper into the world of AI integration in various industries, it becomes evident that the applications of artificial intelligence are as diverse as the sectors themselves. Each industry harnesses AI's capabilities in unique ways, addressing specific challenges and enhancing their operations.

In healthcare, AI's impact is transformative. Applications range from advanced diagnostics, where AI algorithms assist in interpreting medical images, to treatment planning, where AI helps in devising personalized treatment regimens. AI is also revolutionizing patient care management, offering tools for monitoring patient health and predicting medical events before they occur.

The finance sector is leveraging AI for a more secure and personalized customer experience. AI plays a crucial role in risk assessment, analyzing vast amounts of data to identify potential risks in investments. Fraud detection has been enhanced significantly with AI, capable of identifying suspicious activities with greater accuracy. Additionally, AI is used in personalizing banking services, tailoring financial advice, and offerings to individual customer needs.

In the realm of retail, AI is reshaping the way businesses understand and interact with their customers. Through customer behavior analysis, retailers use AI to gain insights into shopping patterns, enhancing their marketing strategies. AI-driven inventory management systems are optimizing stock levels and supply chain logistics. Personalized shopping experiences, powered by AI, are becoming increasingly prevalent, offering customers recommendations based on their preferences and purchase history.

Manufacturing has seen substantial efficiency gains through the adoption of AI. Predictive maintenance, enabled by AI, allows for timely maintenance of machinery, reducing downtime. AI systems are used in quality control processes, identifying defects and irregularities with high precision. Moreover, AI plays a key role in supply chain optimization, predicting demand, and streamlining production schedules.

In creative industries, AI's influence is reshaping content creation and design. AI algorithms are being used to generate new content, from writing articles to composing music. In the field of design, AI assists in creating visual elements, offering new possibilities in digital media and advertising.

These diverse applications across industries demonstrate the versatility and transformative potential of AI. As we explore these examples, the depth of AI's integration and its implications for each sector become increasingly clear. These case studies not only highlight the innovative uses of AI but also shed light on the broader impact of its integration on industry-specific workflows and the global economy.

In healthcare, AI's potential to enhance patient care has been increasingly recognized and realized. One notable success story is that of a healthcare organization which implemented AI to revolutionize its patient care system.

This organization faced challenges common in the healthcare industry: an overwhelming amount of patient data and the need for rapid, accurate diagnosis and treatment plans. To address these challenges, the organization integrated AI into its operations, focusing on two key areas: diagnostics and patient care management.

In diagnostics, the organization used AI algorithms to analyze medical imaging. These AI systems were trained on vast datasets of images, enabling them to assist doctors in identifying diseases such as cancer at much earlier stages than previously possible. The AI's ability to recognize patterns undetectable to the human eye significantly improved diagnostic accuracy and efficiency.

In patient care management, the organization utilized AI to monitor patient data in real-time. AI systems analyzed data from various sources, including medical records and real-time monitoring devices, to predict potential health risks. This proactive approach allowed healthcare providers to intervene earlier, often preventing medical emergencies.

The implementation of AI led to remarkable improvements in patient outcomes. The accuracy and speed of diagnostics increased, and the efficiency of patient care management improved, leading to higher patient satisfaction rates. Moreover, the AI systems provided valuable insights that helped the organization streamline its operations and reduce costs.

This case study demonstrates the profound impact that AI can have in healthcare when successfully adopted. By leveraging AI's capabilities, the organization not only enhanced its patient care but also set a benchmark for innovation in healthcare services.

The integration of AI in the financial sector has brought about significant enhancements in customer service and security, as illustrated in the case study of a prominent financial institution. This institution faced the dual challenge of meeting ever-increasing customer service expectations while ensuring robust security against fraud and financial crimes.

To tackle these challenges, the institution implemented AI in several key areas. Firstly, they introduced AI-powered chatbots and virtual assistants to their customer service channels. These AI tools were equipped to handle a wide range of customer inquiries, from account balance queries to transaction assistance. Utilizing natural language processing and machine learning, the chatbots provided timely, personalized responses, greatly enhancing the customer experience. They also reduced the workload on human customer service representatives, allowing them to focus on more complex customer issues.

In terms of security, the institution employed AI for advanced fraud detection and risk assessment. The AI system was designed to analyze transaction patterns and flag any unusual or suspicious activities, a task that would be cumbersome and less effective if done manually. By learning from historical transaction data, the AI model became increasingly adept at identifying potential fraud, thereby significantly reducing the incidence of financial crimes.

AI was used for personalized banking services. The AI algorithms analyzed individual customer data to offer customized financial advice and product recommendations. This personalization not only improved customer satisfaction but also increased the efficiency of the institution's marketing efforts.

The successful implementation of AI in customer service and security brought about several key benefits. Customer engagement and satisfaction saw a marked improvement due to the quick and personalized responses provided by the AI chatbots. The efficiency and accuracy in fraud detection enhanced the institution's security measures, instilling greater trust in their customers. Additionally, the operational efficiency gained through AI integration resulted in cost savings and an improved bottom line.

This case study exemplifies the transformative potential of AI in the financial sector, showcasing how the thoughtful application of AI can simultaneously enhance customer experience and bolster security measures.

A leading retail giant provides a compelling case study of how AI can be leveraged for inventory and customer relationship management, revolutionizing the retail sector's approach to business operations and consumer engagement.

Faced with the challenges of managing a vast and dynamic inventory across numerous locations and predicting consumer trends accurately, the retail giant turned to AI for solutions. They implemented an AI-driven inventory management system that utilized predictive analytics to forecast demand, optimize stock levels, and manage supply chain logistics. The AI system analyzed sales data, seasonal trends, and consumer behavior to predict which products would be in demand at various times of the year. This predictive capability allowed the company to optimize stock levels, minimizing overstock and understock situations, leading to significant cost savings and reduced waste.

In customer relationship management, the retail giant employed AI to personalize the shopping experience for its customers. They used AI algorithms to analyze customer purchase history, browsing behavior, and preferences. Based on this data, the AI system provided personalized product recommendations to customers both in-store and online. This personalization was not limited to product recommendations; it also extended to marketing campaigns and promotional offers, tailored to the individual preferences of each customer.

The company implemented AI-powered chatbots on their website and mobile app, providing customers with 24/7 assistance. These chatbots were capable of handling a range of queries, from product inquiries to order tracking, enhancing the overall customer experience.

The integration of AI into inventory and customer relationship management had a transformative impact on the retail giant's operations. The efficiency of inventory management improved significantly, resulting in cost savings and a better ability to meet consumer demand. The personalized shopping experience led to increased customer satisfaction, higher sales, and enhanced customer loyalty. Additionally, the AI-driven insights helped the company in strategizing and making data-backed decisions to stay ahead in the competitive retail market.

This case study exemplifies the power of AI in optimizing business operations and elevating the customer experience in the retail sector. By leveraging AI for inventory management and customer relationship management, the retail giant not only streamlined its operations but also established a stronger connection with its customers.

The integration of AI into organizational operations, while transformative, often comes with its set of challenges. These hurdles can range from technical and infrastructural issues to human resource and ethical concerns. Understanding and addressing these challenges is crucial for successful AI adoption.

One common challenge faced by organizations is the technical complexity involved in developing or implementing AI systems. This includes the need for significant investment in technology and infrastructure, as well as the challenge of integrating AI with existing systems and processes. Additionally, there is often a skills gap; many organizations lack the in-house expertise necessary to develop, manage, and interpret AI technologies effectively.

Data-related challenges are also prevalent. These include acquiring high-quality, relevant data to train AI models, ensuring data privacy, and managing large volumes of data securely. Moreover, biases in data can lead to skewed AI outputs, raising concerns about fairness and accuracy.

From a human resource perspective, resistance to change among employees can be a hurdle. There can be apprehensions about job security or skepticism about the efficacy of AI systems. Additionally, there is the challenge of upskilling the workforce to work effectively with AI technologies. Organizations have adopted various strategies to overcome these challenges. To address technical complexity and the skills gap, many companies are partnering with AI technology providers or investing in employee training and development. Collaborations with universities and research institutions are also common for gaining access to cutting-edge AI expertise and resources.

For data-related challenges, organizations are focusing on developing robust data governance policies. This involves not only ensuring data quality and privacy but also actively working to identify and eliminate biases in data sets. Regular audits and reviews of AI systems are also being conducted to ensure fairness and accuracy.

To tackle resistance to change, organizations are adopting a proactive approach to change management. This includes clear communication about the benefits of AI, involving employees in the AI integration process, and providing reassurances about job security and upskilling opportunities.

The exploration of AI integration across various industries, through diverse case studies, has yielded valuable lessons and insights. These learnings are not only crucial for understanding the potential of AI but also for navigating the challenges that come with its implementation. Summarizing these key learnings offers a set of best practices and recommendations, aiding organizations in their journey towards successful AI integration.

From the healthcare sector to retail and finance, one of the key lessons is the importance of aligning AI initiatives with specific organizational goals and needs. Successful AI integration begins with a clear understanding of what the organization aims to achieve – be it enhanced customer experience, improved operational efficiency, or innovation in product and service offerings.

Data quality and management emerge as critical factors. The case studies underscore the need for high-quality, diverse, and representative data to train AI models. This ensures that AI systems are accurate, fair, and effective. Organizations must invest in robust data governance frameworks to address issues of privacy, security, and bias.

The human aspect of AI integration, particularly change management, is another vital lesson. It's crucial to address employee apprehensions and involve them in the AI adoption process. This can be achieved through transparent communication, offering reassurance about job security, and providing training and upskilling opportunities. Another significant learning is the necessity of maintaining ethical standards in AI deployment. This involves developing ethical guidelines, ensuring transparency in AI operations, and continuous monitoring for biases and ethical lapses. Ethical AI use not only builds trust among stakeholders but also ensures long-term sustainability of AI initiatives.

Technical expertise and partnerships are also key. Many successful case studies involved collaborations with tech partners, academic institutions, or specialized AI vendors. These partnerships can provide the necessary technical expertise and resources that might be lacking in-house. Scalability and flexibility in AI solutions are important. AI systems should be scalable to grow with the organization and flexible enough to adapt to changing market dynamics and business needs. The best practices for successful AI integration include aligning AI with business goals, ensuring robust data governance, managing the human aspects of AI adoption, maintaining ethical standards, leveraging partnerships for technical expertise, and focusing on scalability and flexibility. These recommendations provide a roadmap for organizations across industries to effectively harness the benefits of AI while navigating its challenges.

As we look towards the future, the potential applications of AI seem boundless, and its role in driving growth and innovation across industries is unmistakable. The road ahead for AI integration is marked by a landscape of continuous evolution, where adaptation and innovation are not just beneficial but essential for success.

The potential future applications of AI are vast and varied. In healthcare, we might see AI further revolutionizing personalized medicine, enabling treatments tailored to the genetic makeup of individual patients. In the realm of environmental science, AI could play a critical role in climate modeling and in developing solutions for sustainable living. The financial sector might witness even more sophisticated AI-driven algorithms for predictive market analysis and personalized financial planning.
In sectors like manufacturing and logistics, AI could lead to fully autonomous supply chains and smart manufacturing processes, enhancing efficiency and reducing operational costs. Retail and e-commerce are likely to see further advancements in AI-driven

customer experience, with hyper-personalized shopping and predictive analytics shaping consumer trends.

The importance of continuous innovation in AI integration cannot be overstated. As technology evolves, so too must the strategies for its integration. This means staying abreast of the latest developments in AI, experimenting with new applications, and being open to redefining business processes in light of AI advancements. It also involves investing in research and development and fostering a culture of innovation within organizations.

Adaptation is equally crucial. As AI technologies and applications evolve, so do the challenges associated with them, including ethical considerations, data privacy, and workforce impact. Organizations must be agile in adapting their policies, strategies, and operations to address these challenges. This includes regularly reviewing and updating AI systems, reevaluating ethical guidelines, and ensuring that the workforce is equipped with the skills necessary to work alongside advancing AI technologies.

The future of AI integration is not a linear path but a dynamic journey of exploration, innovation, and adaptation. For organizations willing to embrace this journey, AI presents unparalleled opportunities for growth, efficiency, and competitiveness. As we move forward, the ability to innovate and adapt will be key determinants in harnessing the full potential of AI for future growth. We have journeyed through a spectrum of industries, each showcasing the transformative impact of AI in real-world settings. These case studies not only provide concrete examples of AI's capabilities but also bring to light the complexities and nuances of integrating such advanced technology into various sectors.

From healthcare to finance, retail to manufacturing, each case study has offered unique insights into the practical applications of AI. We've seen how AI can enhance efficiency, drive innovation, and personalize customer experiences. At the same time, these examples have highlighted challenges such as managing data privacy, addressing AI bias, and ensuring ethical AI usage.

Connecting these insights to the broader narrative of AI's impact on work culture and hybrid work models, it becomes clear that AI is not just a tool for operational efficiency. Its influence extends to reshaping job roles, necessitating new skill sets, and redefining the dynamics of the workplace. In hybrid work models, AI's role in facilitating communication, automating processes, and providing data-driven insights is pivotal in bridging the gap between physical and virtual work environments.

The lessons learned from these case studies emphasize the importance of strategic AI integration, considering not just the technological aspects but also the human and ethical dimensions. They underscore the need for continuous learning, adaptability, and ethical vigilance as AI becomes more ingrained in our professional lives.

The case studies in this chapter have provided a microcosm of AI's broader impact on the workplace. They serve as both a guide and a cautionary tale for organizations embarking on their AI journey, highlighting the potential rewards and the challenges to be navigated. As we move forward in this era of AI integration, the insights gained from these real-world examples will be invaluable in shaping a future where AI enhances work culture, optimizes hybrid work models, and drives sustainable growth.

# Part 2: Navigating Hybrid Workplace Models

In Part 2, we shift our focus to the evolving landscape of hybrid workplace models. As the world of work embraces flexibility and technological integration, understanding and navigating this new terrain becomes essential for organizations and employees alike. This section of the book investigates the rise of hybrid work, its historical context, the technology driving it, and the strategies for effective management in such environments.

We begin by exploring the rise of hybrid work, tracing its origins and the recent surge in its adoption. This exploration isn't just a historical account; it's a journey through the evolving needs and expectations of the modern workforce and the organizational responses to these changes. We discuss the various advantages of hybrid models, such as increased flexibility and potential for improved work-life balance, while also confronting the challenges, including issues of connectivity, team cohesion, and maintaining company culture.

Technology and infrastructure are the backbone of effective hybrid workplaces. In this context, we review the essential technologies that make remote collaboration not only possible but productive. We look at how virtual workspaces are created and maintained, and the importance of cybersecurity in a hybrid model, where data and information flow across multiple networks and devices.

Managing remote teams in hybrid settings requires an adaptive leadership style. We delve into how leadership in remote settings is distinct from traditional office management, focusing on engagement strategies to keep remote employees motivated and performance management to ensure productivity and accountability.

Finally, we bring these concepts to life with case studies from organizations that have successfully implemented hybrid workplace models. These real-world examples provide unique insights into how different organizations navigate the transition, the innovations they bring to the practice, and the valuable lessons they've learned along the way.

Part 2 serves as a comprehensive guide for navigating the complex yet rewarding world of hybrid work models. It provides the tools, strategies, and insights necessary for businesses and individuals to adapt, thrive, and maintain resilience in an increasingly flexible and digitized work environment.

# Chapter 5: The Rise of Hybrid Work

As we transition into Chapter 5 of "The Future of Work Now," we turn our attention to the evolving concept of hybrid work models. This introductory section provides a brief overview of what constitutes a hybrid work model, laying the foundation for understanding its increasing prominence and relevance in today's work culture.

Hybrid work models represent a blend of traditional office-based work and remote work. In such models, employees have the flexibility to divide their time between working in an office environment and working remotely – be it from home, a co-working space, or another location. This approach to work is a significant shift from the conventional 9-to-5 office setup, offering a more flexible and adaptable working arrangement.

The rise of hybrid work models can be attributed to several factors, including advancements in technology, changing employee expectations, and the global shift in work practices triggered by events like the COVID-19 pandemic. These models have gained popularity as they offer a balance between the structure and collaboration opportunities of in-office work and the flexibility and autonomy of remote work. These models are not one-size-fits-all; they vary significantly from organization to organization. Some may opt for a structured approach, with set days for in-office and remote work, while others may offer more flexibility, allowing employees to choose their work location based on their needs and preferences.

We will explore the nuances of hybrid work models, examining how they are reshaping the work environment, the benefits and challenges they present, and their implications for the future of work. The rise of hybrid work models marks a significant evolution in work culture, reflecting the changing dynamics of the modern workplace and the ongoing shift towards more dynamic and flexible work practices.

The concept of hybrid work, while gaining unprecedented prominence recently, has its roots in the early practices of flexible working arrangements. This historical context is essential to understand how work models have evolved from traditional office settings to the dynamic arrangements we see today.

The origins of flexible work can be traced back to the 1970s and 1980s when businesses began experimenting with alternative work arrangements such as flextime and job sharing. These early concepts were driven by a desire to increase employee satisfaction and productivity while balancing work and personal life. The advent of the digital age in the late 20th century further fueled the possibility of working outside the traditional office environment.

The significant technological milestone that made hybrid work a viable option was the proliferation of the internet and mobile technology. The late 1990s and early 2000s saw a rapid advancement in digital communication tools, cloud computing, and mobile devices, enabling workers to perform their tasks from anywhere with an internet connection. This technological revolution laid the groundwork for remote working as a feasible and efficient option.

Social changes also played a key role in the evolution of work models. The increasing focus on work-life balance, particularly among the millennial and Gen Z workforce, has been a driving force in the shift towards more flexible work arrangements. Additionally, environmental considerations, such as reducing commuting and the associated carbon footprint, have also influenced this shift.

The concept of hybrid work gained significant momentum with the advent of the COVID-19 pandemic. The global health crisis forced businesses worldwide to adopt remote working arrangements almost overnight. This unplanned mass experiment in remote work demonstrated the feasibility of flexible work models on a large scale and led to a reevaluation of the necessity of traditional office-centric work.

The evolution of hybrid work models is the result of a confluence of technological advancements, social changes, and global events. These factors have collectively paved the way for the adoption of more flexible, dynamic work arrangements, challenging the traditional norms of how and where work is done. As we explore further in this chapter, the historical context of hybrid work provides a lens through which to view its current state and future potential.

The recent surge in the adoption of hybrid work models represents a significant shift in the global work landscape. Several factors have contributed to this increase, fundamentally reshaping how organizations and employees view the concept of work.

A primary catalyst for the rapid transition to hybrid work models has been the impact of global events, most notably the COVID-19 pandemic. The pandemic forced businesses and employees to quickly adapt to remote working as governments-imposed lockdowns and social distancing measures. This unplanned shift demonstrated the feasibility of remote work on a large scale, challenging long-held beliefs about productivity and collaboration in traditional office settings. As a result, many organizations and employees began to see the potential benefits of flexible work arrangements, leading to a growing interest in hybrid models as a more permanent solution.

Another factor contributing to the rise of hybrid work is the advancement in digital technologies. The availability of robust communication tools, cloud computing, and collaborative software has made it easier than ever for employees to work effectively from remote locations. These technologies have enabled seamless communication and collaboration, regardless of physical location, making hybrid work models more practical and attractive.

Insights from recent surveys and studies reinforce the growing adoption of hybrid work models globally. Many of these studies indicate a preference among employees for work models that offer flexibility in terms of location and hours. For instance, surveys have shown that a significant percentage of the workforce prefers a mix of remote and in-office work, citing benefits such as improved work-life balance, reduced commute times, and increased productivity.

Organizations are also recognizing the benefits of hybrid work models. These benefits include access to a wider talent pool, reduced overhead costs associated with maintaining large office spaces, and the ability to quickly adapt to changing circumstances, such as public health crises. Additionally, hybrid models can contribute to employee satisfaction and retention by offering the flexibility that modern workers increasingly seek.

The recent surge in hybrid work models is the result of a combination of global events, technological advancements, and changing attitudes towards work. As businesses and employees navigate the post-pandemic world, hybrid work models are becoming an integral part of the new normal, offering a balanced approach that meets the needs of both employers and employees. This chapter aims to delve deeper into these trends, providing a comprehensive view of the current state and future prospects of hybrid work models.

Hybrid work models, blending remote and in-office work, offer a spectrum of benefits for both employees and employers. These advantages are reshaping traditional notions of work, leading to more flexible, efficient, and satisfying work environments.

For employees, one of the most significant benefits of hybrid work arrangements is the improved work-life balance. The flexibility to work remotely reduces the need for daily commuting, freeing up time that can be spent on personal pursuits or with family. This flexibility also allows employees to work during their most productive hours, accommodating individual work styles and preferences. Moreover, the autonomy that comes with hybrid work can lead to increased job satisfaction, as employees feel more in control of their work environment and schedule.

Reduced commute times are another major advantage for employees. Commuting can be both time-consuming and stressful, impacting an employee's overall well-being and productivity. The hybrid model, by allowing remote work, can significantly reduce or even eliminate the daily commute for many employees, leading to less stress and a better quality of life.

For employers, hybrid work models offer their own set of benefits. One of the most notable is the reduction in overhead costs. With employees spending part of their time working remotely, there is less need for large office spaces, which can result in considerable savings on rent, utilities, and other office-related expenses. Additionally, by embracing hybrid models, employers can access a wider talent pool. Geographic limitations become less of a barrier, enabling companies to hire the best talent from anywhere in the world.

Many organizations report potential increases in productivity with the adoption of hybrid work models. The flexibility and autonomy provided by these models can lead to more engaged and motivated employees, which often translates into higher productivity. The ability to work remotely can also reduce workplace distractions, allowing for deeper focus and efficiency in tasks.

The advantages of hybrid work models are manifold, offering significant benefits to both employees and employers. For employees, these include improved work-life balance, reduced commute times, and increased autonomy. For employers, the benefits encompass reduced overhead costs, access to a broader talent pool, and potential increases in productivity. As organizations continue to navigate the post-pandemic world, the adoption and refinement of hybrid work models are likely to play a key role in shaping the future of work.

Hybrid work models, while offering numerous benefits, also present unique challenges and obstacles that organizations must navigate. Identifying and addressing these challenges is crucial for the successful implementation and sustainability of hybrid work arrangements.

One of the primary challenges is maintaining company culture. In a hybrid work environment, where employees are not always physically present in the office, fostering a sense of unity and shared purpose can be difficult. The lack of face-to-face interactions can impact team bonding and the overall organizational culture. To overcome this, companies are finding creative ways to keep their teams connected, such as virtual team-building activities, regular all-hands meetings, and leveraging technology to facilitate informal interactions among employees.

Effective communication is another significant challenge in hybrid work models. Ensuring that all team members, whether working remotely or in the office, are on the same page can be challenging. Miscommunications and information gaps can occur more frequently. Organizations are addressing this by adopting comprehensive communication tools and platforms that facilitate real-time collaboration and information sharing. Regular check-ins, clear communication protocols, and the use of collaborative software help in keeping everyone informed and connected.

Managing remote workforce engagement is another hurdle. Remote employees might feel isolated or disconnected from the broader organizational goals and activities. This can lead to a decrease in engagement and productivity. Solutions to this challenge include offering remote employee opportunities for career growth, recognizing their contributions, and ensuring they have access to the resources and support they need. Regular feedback and engagement surveys can also help in understanding the needs and challenges of remote employees.

Another challenge is ensuring fairness and equity between remote and in-office employees. There's a risk of a two-tier system where in-office employees have more visibility and access to opportunities compared to their remote counterparts. To mitigate this, organizations are striving to create policies and practices that ensure equal treatment, access, and opportunities for all employees, regardless of their work location.

While the transition to hybrid work models comes with challenges such as maintaining company culture, effective communication, and managing remote workforce engagement, there are strategies and solutions to address these issues. By focusing on connectivity, communication, engagement, and equity, organizations can successfully overcome these challenges and harness the full potential of hybrid work models.

Balancing the advantages and challenges of hybrid work models is crucial for organizations seeking to optimize the benefits while mitigating the downsides. This requires a strategic approach that acknowledges and addresses the complexities of hybrid work environments.

One key strategy is to develop a clear and comprehensive hybrid work policy. This policy should outline expectations, provide guidelines on work arrangements, and address issues like communication protocols, performance evaluation, and work-life balance. Having clear policies helps in setting standards and ensuring that all employees, whether working remotely or in the office, are aware of their responsibilities and entitlements.

Effective use of technology is another critical factor in balancing the advantages and challenges of hybrid work. Organizations should invest in the right tools and platforms that facilitate collaboration, communication, and productivity regardless of physical location. This includes project management tools, communication platforms, and secure cloud-based systems for data access and storage. The right technology stack can bridge the gap between remote and in-office employees, fostering a more cohesive and efficient work environment.

Creating opportunities for regular face-to-face interactions, whether in-person or virtually, is important for maintaining a strong company culture and team cohesion. Regular team meetings, virtual check-ins, and occasional in-person gatherings (if feasible) can help in building connections and ensuring that all team members feel included and valued.

Another strategy is to focus on results rather than hours worked. Shifting the focus from traditional measures of productivity, like time spent in the office, to actual outcomes and results can be more effective in a hybrid work environment. This approach requires setting clear goals and performance metrics that are fair and achievable for both remote and in-office employees.

Fostering a culture of trust and flexibility is also essential. Trusting employees to manage their work and time effectively is key in a hybrid work model. Flexibility in work arrangements can contribute to employee satisfaction and productivity, as long as it aligns with organizational goals and customer needs. Continuous feedback and adaptation are crucial in balancing the pros and cons of hybrid work. Organizations should regularly solicit feedback from employees on what is working and what is not and be prepared to adapt and refine their hybrid work strategies accordingly.

As we contemplate the future of hybrid work models, it's clear that current trajectories and technological advancements are paving the way for a more flexible and dynamic work environment. Predicting future trends in this area involves understanding how these elements will continue to evolve and shape the workplace.

One key trend likely to continue is the increasing customization of hybrid work models. As organizations become more experienced with hybrid arrangements, they will likely tailor these models to fit their unique needs, industry demands, and workforce preferences. This could mean a greater variety of hybrid work setups, from fully flexible models where employees choose their work location freely, to more structured arrangements with designated in-office and remote working days.

Technological advancements will continue to play a critical role in the future of hybrid work. Emerging technologies like artificial intelligence, augmented reality, and virtual reality are expected to further enhance remote collaboration, making it more interactive and immersive. These technologies could bridge the gap between physical and virtual workspaces, providing a more seamless experience for employees regardless of their location.

The role of ongoing innovation in shaping the future of hybrid workplaces cannot be overstated. As new technologies emerge and existing ones improve, organizations will have more tools at their disposal to enhance communication, collaboration, and productivity in hybrid work settings. This ongoing innovation will also require continuous adaptation and learning from both employers and employees.

The future of hybrid work will likely see an increased focus on employee well-being and work-life balance. The lessons learned during the rapid shift to remote work during the pandemic have highlighted the importance of supporting the mental and physical health of employees. Future hybrid models may incorporate more wellness-oriented practices and policies, recognizing that employee well-being is integral to productivity and job satisfaction. This model of work is poised for continued evolution, driven by technological advancements and ongoing innovation. These models will become more customized, with a growing emphasis on creating work environments that are both productive and supportive of employee well-being. As organizations navigate this future, adaptability and a willingness to embrace new ways of working will be key to success in the hybrid work landscape.

We have uncovered key insights that delineate the current state and potential future of this evolving work paradigm. This chapter has highlighted the transformative impact that hybrid work models have on both employees and organizations, offering a nuanced understanding of their benefits, challenges, and the strategies to balance them effectively.

The shift towards hybrid work models represents a significant change in how work is perceived and conducted. We've seen how these models offer improved work-life balance, increased autonomy for employees, and potential cost savings for employers. At the same time, they pose unique challenges in maintaining company culture, ensuring effective communication, and managing a dispersed workforce.

Looking ahead, the future of hybrid work seems poised for further evolution, shaped by ongoing technological innovations and a growing emphasis on customization and employee well-being. The adaptability and resilience shown by organizations and employees in embracing hybrid work models indicate a readiness to continue this evolution.

As we transition to the next chapter, our focus shifts to the technology and infrastructure necessary for effective hybrid work environments. This upcoming chapter will delve into the tools and systems that facilitate remote collaboration, communication, and productivity. It will explore how technological advancements are enabling more seamless and efficient hybrid work experiences, and what organizations need to consider in building and maintaining the infrastructure that supports a flexible, hybrid workforce.

# Chapter 6: Technology and Infrastructure for Hybrid Work

The shift towards hybrid work models has been significantly enabled by advancements in technology. In today's world, technology is not just a facilitator but a critical enabler of remote and hybrid work models. It bridges the gap between physical offices and remote work settings, ensuring that teams can collaborate effectively, regardless of their location.

In this chapter, we explore various technological tools and platforms that have become indispensable in hybrid work environments. This includes a range of solutions from cloud computing services that allow employees to access work files and applications remotely, to communication and collaboration tools like video conferencing and project management software, which enable teams to stay connected and productive. The right technology can transform remote work from a mere necessity to a dynamic and interactive experience, paralleling or even surpassing the efficiency of traditional office work.

Understanding the technological infrastructure of hybrid work also involves recognizing the challenges and barriers to its implementation. This includes addressing issues such as cybersecurity, data privacy, and ensuring equitable access to technology for all employees.

As we proceed, this chapter aims to provide a holistic view of the technologies that underpin hybrid work models, examining how they can be optimally deployed to create a cohesive, productive, and secure work environment. The insights gained here are pivotal for organizations looking to navigate the complexities of hybrid work and leverage technology to its fullest potential in this new era of work.

In the landscape of hybrid work, certain technologies have emerged as essential for facilitating collaboration and productivity. These tools and platforms are integral in bridging the gap between remote and in-office environments, ensuring that teams can function seamlessly regardless of their physical location.

A key component of this technological toolkit is communication tools. Video conferencing software, such as Zoom or Microsoft Teams, has become ubiquitous in the hybrid work model, allowing for face-to-face meetings without the need for physical presence. These tools also often include features like chat functions, file sharing, and screen sharing, further enhancing their utility for collaborative work.

Project management software is another crucial element in the hybrid work environment. Tools like Asana, Trello, or Jira help teams track progress, manage tasks, and collaborate on projects in real-time. They provide a centralized platform where team members can see updates, deadlines, and deliverables, which is particularly important when team members are not physically together. Cloud-based solutions form the backbone of hybrid work's technological infrastructure. Cloud storage and computing services like Google Drive, Dropbox, or AWS enable employees to access and work on documents and applications from any location, fostering a flexible and mobile work environment. The cloud also facilitates data syncing, ensuring that all team members have access to the latest versions of documents and resources.

The integration of these technologies into daily work processes is crucial for ensuring effective collaboration in a hybrid work setting. This requires not just the deployment of these tools but also training for employees to use them effectively. It also involves setting up protocols and best practices for their use, such as guidelines for communication, data storage, and project management.

The integration of these tools should be done with an eye towards creating a cohesive digital workspace. This means ensuring that the various tools are compatible with each other and can be easily accessed through a unified interface. The goal is to create an environment where transitioning from in-office to remote work, and vice versa, is as smooth and frictionless as possible. The essential technologies for hybrid work encompass communication tools, project management software, and cloud-based solutions. The effective integration of these technologies into daily work processes is key to realizing the full potential of hybrid work models. As we explore these technologies further, we will jump into how they can be optimized to support a productive, efficient, and connected hybrid workforce.

The concept of a virtual workspace has become increasingly relevant in the era of hybrid work, where the physical boundaries of traditional offices are extended into the digital realm. A virtual workspace refers to an online environment that replicates or enhances aspects of a physical office, providing a platform for employees to interact, collaborate, and complete their tasks regardless of their physical location.

Creating effective virtual workspaces involves more than just providing the right tools and technologies; it requires thoughtful strategies to ensure these environments are conducive to productivity and collaboration. Key to this is the creation of a digital space that is organized, engaging, and accessible, fostering a sense of community among remote team members.
One strategy is to ensure that virtual workspaces are well-structured and easy to navigate. This can involve organizing digital files and resources in a logical manner, using project management tools to clearly define tasks and responsibilities, and ensuring that communication channels are established and understood by all team members. Virtual workspaces should also be equipped with collaborative tools that enable real-time communication and collaboration, such as shared digital whiteboards, document collaboration platforms, and instant messaging systems.

Another important aspect is maintaining a sense of presence and engagement among team members. Regular video meetings, virtual team-building activities, and informal virtual gatherings can help maintain team cohesion and morale. Additionally, ensuring that all team members have equal access to information and opportunities to contribute is vital in preventing feelings of isolation or exclusion.

The use of virtual reality (VR) and augmented reality (AR) technologies presents exciting possibilities for enhancing remote work experiences. VR can create immersive virtual environments where employees can interact as if they were in the same physical space, which can be particularly useful for activities like brainstorming sessions, training programs, or simulating work scenarios. AR, on the other hand, can overlay digital information onto the physical world, aiding in tasks like virtual equipment repair or providing real-time data overlays for complex tasks.

These advanced technologies can make remote collaboration more interactive and engaging, bridging the gap between physical and digital workspaces. However, their implementation requires careful consideration of factors such as cost, accessibility, and the specific needs of the organization and its employees. Building effective virtual workspaces is a multifaceted endeavor. It involves creating a structured and engaging digital environment, equipped with the right tools for collaboration and communication, and potentially enhanced by advanced technologies like VR and AR. As we delve deeper into this topic, we explore how virtual workspaces can be optimized to support a productive, efficient, and cohesive remote workforce.

The success of hybrid work models heavily relies on reliable internet connectivity and accessibility for remote workers. Consistent and high-quality connectivity is not just a convenience but a necessity for ensuring productivity and smooth collaboration in a hybrid work environment. Reliable internet connectivity is fundamental for remote workers to effectively access virtual workspaces, use collaboration tools, and communicate with team members. Poor connectivity can lead to interrupted communications, delays in project timelines, and a general decrease in productivity. It can also cause frustration and disengagement among team members, impacting the overall team dynamics and work culture.

To ensure consistent and high-quality connectivity for their workforce, organizations can adopt several best practices:

1. Providing Necessary Hardware and Software: Organizations can equip their remote workforce with the necessary hardware, such as laptops, smartphones, and perhaps even Wi-Fi extenders or signal boosters. They can also provide software solutions that optimize bandwidth usage and ensure secure connections.

2. Supporting Home Office Setups: Offering stipends or reimbursements for home office setups can encourage employees to invest in high-quality internet services. Organizations might also consider providing guidelines or recommendations for setting up an efficient home workspace.

3. VPN and Secure Network Access: Ensuring that employees have access to a secure Virtual Private Network (VPN) is crucial for protecting company data and maintaining privacy. This is especially important for organizations handling sensitive information.

4. Flexible Working Hours: Recognizing that internet connectivity might vary throughout the day, especially in shared or residential areas, offering flexible working hours can allow employees to work when their internet connection is most stable.

5. Training and Technical Support: Providing training on best practices for maintaining a stable internet connection and offering readily available technical support can help employees troubleshoot connectivity issues quickly.

6. Regular Connectivity Checks: Encouraging regular connectivity checks or audits can help identify and address potential issues before they impact work.

7. Investing in Technology Infrastructure: For some organizations, investing in improved technology infrastructure, such as enhanced cloud capabilities or dedicated communication platforms, can offer more stable and efficient connectivity solutions for their workforce.

By focusing on these best practices, organizations can ensure that their remote and hybrid workforce remains connected and productive. Reliable internet connectivity and accessibility are key enablers of effective hybrid work models, and as such, they require careful attention and investment.

In a hybrid work model, where employees split their time between remote locations and the office, cybersecurity challenges become more complex and multifaceted. The dispersed nature of the workforce increases the potential for security vulnerabilities, making it imperative for organizations to adopt robust security measures and protocols.

One of the primary cybersecurity challenges in hybrid work environments is the increased risk of data breaches and cyber-attacks. Remote work often relies on personal or less secure networks, which can be more susceptible to breaches than secured office networks. Additionally, the use of personal devices for work purposes can pose risks if these devices are not properly secured.

To address these challenges, organizations need to implement comprehensive security measures and protocols. This includes the use of secure Virtual Private Networks (VPNs) to protect data transmission, employing firewalls and antivirus software, and ensuring secure access to company systems through multi-factor authentication and strong password policies. Another critical aspect of cybersecurity in a hybrid work model is the protection of sensitive data. Organizations should consider data encryption both in transit and at rest and implement strict access controls to ensure that only authorized personnel have access to sensitive information. Regular security audits and vulnerability assessments can help identify and address potential security gaps.

Employee training and awareness are also vital components of a robust cybersecurity strategy. Employees need to be educated about common cyber threats, such as phishing attacks, and how to recognize and report them. Training should also cover safe internet practices, the importance of regular software updates, and guidelines for using personal devices for work.

Organizations should develop and communicate clear cybersecurity policies and protocols. These policies should outline the responsibilities of employees in maintaining security, provide guidance on secure remote work practices, and establish procedures for responding to security incidents. Creating a culture of cybersecurity awareness is essential. Regular communication about security threats and reminders of best practices can help keep cybersecurity at the forefront of employees' minds. Involving employees in security planning and feedback can also enhance their commitment to following security protocols.

Cybersecurity in a hybrid work model requires a comprehensive approach that combines technology solutions with employee training and awareness. By implementing robust security measures, educating employees, and fostering a culture of security mindfulness, organizations can protect their data and systems against the increased risks presented by hybrid work environments.

In hybrid work settings, certain technological hurdles can impede the smooth operation and efficiency of the workforce. Identifying and overcoming these challenges is crucial to ensure that all team members, regardless of their location, have the necessary tools and resources to perform their jobs effectively.

One common hurdle is the issue of inconsistent technology experiences between the office and remote environments. Employees working remotely may not have access to the same level of technology and resources as those in the office, which can lead to disparities in work efficiency and collaboration. To overcome this, organizations can standardize the technology and tools used across the board. Providing remote employees with the same hardware and software used in the office can ensure a consistent work experience.

Another challenge is the lack of adequate technical support for remote employees. When technical issues arise, remote workers might not have immediate access to in-house IT support. Solutions include establishing a robust remote IT support system, offering virtual help desks, and providing clear guidelines and resources for troubleshooting common issues. Connectivity issues are also a significant barrier in hybrid work environments. Ensuring stable and secure internet connections for remote workers is essential. Solutions can include providing stipends for high-quality home internet services, offering mobile hotspots, or implementing technologies that optimize bandwidth usage for remote work.

Some employees may lack the skills or knowledge to use new technologies effectively, leading to underutilization and inefficiencies. To address this, organizations can invest in comprehensive training programs that are tailored to the needs of their workforce. These programs should cover not only the basics of using the technology but also best practices for remote collaboration and security. Ensuring equitable access to technology is also crucial. Organizations should assess the specific needs of their employees, including those with disabilities, to provide appropriate accommodations and tools that support an inclusive work environment.

Navigating the integration of various technologies can be overwhelming for employees. A unified platform or interface that integrates various tools and applications can simplify the technology landscape for users, making it easier to access and use different tools effectively. Overcoming technological barriers in hybrid work settings involves ensuring consistency in technology experiences, providing robust remote IT support, addressing connectivity issues, offering comprehensive training, ensuring equitable access, and simplifying the integration of various technologies. By implementing these solutions and strategies, organizations can create a more efficient, inclusive, and collaborative hybrid work environment.

The evolution of hybrid work models has significantly transformed the role of IT support, making it more crucial and complex. In a hybrid environment, where employees are dispersed between office settings and remote locations, the demands on IT support are diverse and often require innovative solutions. The changing role of IT support in a hybrid work model includes not just addressing technical issues but also proactively managing the technology infrastructure to ensure smooth operations. IT teams must be equipped to handle a range of challenges, from connectivity issues and software troubleshooting to cybersecurity and data management.

One of the best practices for IT teams in providing effective support remotely is the establishment of a robust remote support system. This can include a helpdesk or ticketing system that is accessible to all employees, regardless of their location. This system should be capable of efficiently handling requests, tracking issues, and facilitating quick resolutions.

Another important practice is the implementation of remote monitoring and management tools. These tools allow IT teams to remotely monitor the health and performance of devices and systems, perform maintenance tasks, and address issues before they become significant problems. Remote management tools can also help in administering software updates and security patches, ensuring that all devices are secure and up-to-date.

Training and empowering employees to handle basic troubleshooting themselves can also alleviate the burden on IT support. This can be achieved through regular training sessions, detailed user guides, and self-service resources. Empowering employees with basic IT skills can reduce the volume of support requests and allow IT teams to focus on more complex issues.

Ensuring strong communication channels between IT support and the rest of the organization is also crucial. Regular updates about system changes, maintenance schedules, and cybersecurity threats can help keep all employees informed and vigilant. Additionally, feedback mechanisms should be in place to understand employees' challenges and experiences with the technology, allowing for continuous improvement.

IT support in a hybrid work model also requires flexibility and adaptability. As hybrid work environments continue to evolve, IT teams must be prepared to adapt their strategies and tools to meet changing needs and challenges. This might involve experimenting with new technologies, adjusting support hours to accommodate different time zones, or customizing support for different teams or departments.

The role of IT support in hybrid work models is multifaceted and vital for the smooth functioning of the organization. Effective remote support, proactive system management, employee training, strong communication, and adaptability are key best practices that IT teams should adopt to provide effective support in a hybrid work environment.

As we look towards the future of hybrid work, it's evident that technological advancements will continue to play a pivotal role in shaping these work environments. Anticipating and understanding these advancements is crucial for organizations to remain adaptable and responsive, ensuring that they harness the full potential of technology to enhance hybrid work models.

One of the key areas of future technological advancement is likely to be in communication and collaboration tools. As hybrid work becomes more prevalent, we can expect to see further innovations in these tools to make remote interactions as seamless and engaging as face-to-face meetings. This could include advancements in virtual and augmented reality, offering more immersive meeting experiences, and new platforms that integrate various forms of communication and collaboration more effectively.

Another significant trend could be the increased use of artificial intelligence and machine learning in automating routine tasks and providing data-driven insights. This technology could enable more personalized and efficient work experiences, from automating scheduling and administrative tasks to providing employees with insights to optimize their work processes and productivity.

The importance of cybersecurity will also continue to grow in the context of hybrid work. As the boundaries between office and remote work blur, securing corporate networks and data across multiple locations and devices will become even more critical. We can anticipate advancements in cybersecurity technologies, including more sophisticated encryption methods, advanced threat detection systems, and secure access management solutions.

The infrastructure for remote work is likely to evolve, with further development in cloud technologies and network infrastructure. This evolution could lead to more robust and secure cloud services, higher internet speeds, and more reliable connectivity solutions, making remote work more efficient and accessible.

Staying adaptable and responsive to these emerging technologies is vital for organizations. This requires not only keeping abreast of technological trends but also fostering a culture of innovation and continuous learning within the organization. It also involves regularly reviewing and updating IT infrastructure and policies to incorporate new technologies and ensuring that employees are trained and comfortable with these advancements.

The future of technology for hybrid work is poised for significant advancements, with potential impacts on communication, collaboration, automation, cybersecurity, and infrastructure. For organizations, staying informed, adaptable, and responsive to these changes will be key to leveraging technology effectively in hybrid work models and maintaining a competitive edge in the evolving work landscape.

# Chapter 7: Managing Remote Teams

We will investigate the intricacies of managing remote teams, a critical component of the hybrid and remote work models that have become increasingly prevalent in today's work environment. This introductory section lays the groundwork for understanding the unique nuances and challenges that come with leading and managing teams outside the traditional office setting.

The shift towards remote and hybrid work models has brought to light the need for specialized leadership and management strategies. In a remote work setting, traditional management methods, largely reliant on face-to-face interactions and physical office presence, are no longer entirely effective. Managing remote teams requires a different approach, one that considers the challenges of physical separation, relies heavily on technology for communication, and places a greater emphasis on trust and autonomy.

Remote team management encompasses various aspects, from ensuring effective communication and collaboration to maintaining team morale and productivity. It involves navigating the challenges of different time zones, cultural differences, and individual work styles, all while striving to meet organizational goals and objectives.

Leaders and managers of remote teams must also be adept at using digital tools for team coordination and project management. They need to be proactive in fostering team cohesion and a sense of belonging among team members who may feel isolated due to the lack of in-person interactions.

This chapter sets the stage for exploring various strategies, tools, and best practices in managing remote teams. It aims to provide insights into creating an effective remote work culture, ensuring team productivity, and maintaining employee engagement and satisfaction in a remote or hybrid work environment. As we navigate this chapter, we will uncover the essential skills and approaches needed for successful remote team management in the modern workplace.

Leadership in remote settings demands a shift from traditional styles, adapting to the unique dynamics of remote work environments. Effective leadership in these settings hinges on fostering communication, building trust, and setting a strong example.

Adapting leadership styles for remote environments often means moving away from micromanagement and towards a more trust-based approach. Leaders need to trust their teams to manage their tasks effectively without constant oversight. This shift requires clear communication of expectations and goals, allowing team members autonomy in how they achieve these objectives.

Effective communication is paramount in remote settings. Leaders must ensure that all team members feel connected and informed, despite the lack of face-to-face interaction. This involves regular check-ins, clear and consistent communication channels, and transparent sharing of information. Digital tools like video conferencing, instant messaging, and collaborative platforms play a crucial role in facilitating this communication. Trust-building is another critical aspect of remote leadership. Trust in a remote setting is fostered through consistent actions, reliability, and open communication. Leaders should demonstrate their commitment to team members' success and well-being, showing empathy and understanding for the unique challenges of remote work.

Leading by example is particularly effective in remote settings. Leaders who embrace the tools and practices of remote work set a positive precedent for their teams. This includes adhering to online meeting etiquettes, respecting work-life boundaries, and demonstrating effective remote work practices.

Remote leaders also face specific challenges, such as managing a team spread across different time zones, ensuring equitable participation and visibility for all team members, and maintaining team cohesion. Overcoming these challenges often requires creative solutions such as flexible meeting schedules, rotating meeting times to accommodate different time zones, and creating opportunities for informal virtual interactions to build team camaraderie.

Recognizing and celebrating achievements can be more challenging in a remote setting. Leaders need to find ways to acknowledge individual and team successes, which can be done through virtual shout-outs, recognition in team meetings, or digital reward systems. Leadership in remote settings requires a blend of adapted management styles, effective use of communication tools, trust-building, leading by example, and innovative solutions to unique challenges. By embracing these strategies, leaders can effectively manage and inspire their teams, regardless of physical distances.

Engagement in remote work settings hinges on a unique set of factors, distinct from traditional office environments. Keeping remote employees engaged and connected requires innovative approaches and strategies that address the challenges of physical separation and digital communication. One key factor driving engagement in remote settings is the feeling of being valued and connected to the team and the larger organization. This can be fostered through regular and meaningful communication, recognition of achievements, and opportunities for professional growth and development.

Innovative approaches to engagement in remote settings often involve leveraging technology to create interactive and collaborative experiences. Virtual team-building activities, such as online games, group challenges, or digital workshops, can be effective in breaking the monotony of remote work and fostering team spirit. These activities help in building relationships among team members and creating a sense of belonging.

Another important strategy is implementing regular check-ins and one-on-one meetings. These sessions provide employees with a platform to share their thoughts, challenges, and successes. They also allow managers to offer personalized support and feedback, fostering a two-way communication channel that is essential for engagement.

Providing opportunities for learning and development is also crucial in keeping remote employees engaged. Online training programs, webinars, and workshops can help employees develop new skills and stay updated with industry trends, contributing to their professional growth. Encouraging informal interactions and social connections among team members can further enhance engagement. Creating virtual spaces for casual conversations, like digital coffee breaks or non-work-related chat channels, can replicate the social aspect of an office environment and strengthen team bonds.

Fostering a sense of community among remote employees is another essential aspect. This can be achieved through regular team updates, sharing company news, celebrating milestones and successes, and involving employees in decision-making processes. Ensuring work-life balance is critical in remote settings. Encouraging employees to set boundaries, respect each other's time, and take regular breaks can prevent burnout and maintain overall well-being. Engagement strategies for remote employees should focus on creating a sense of connection, providing opportunities for interaction and growth, and ensuring a healthy work-life balance. By implementing these strategies, organizations can foster a vibrant and engaged remote workforce.

Effective communication is the lifeline of remote teams, playing a critical role in ensuring collaboration, productivity, and team cohesion. In the absence of face-to-face interactions, clear, consistent, and effective communication becomes even more vital.

The importance of clear and consistent communication in remote teams cannot be overstated. It helps in setting expectations, reducing misunderstandings, and keeping team members aligned with their goals and tasks. Effective communication also contributes to a sense of community and belonging among team members, which can otherwise be challenging to achieve in a remote setting.

To maintain open lines of communication, various tools and practices are employed. Video conferencing tools like Zoom or Microsoft Teams facilitate face-to-face interactions and real-time discussions, which are essential for complex or sensitive conversations. Instant messaging platforms such as Slack or Microsoft Teams provide a space for quick, informal chats and updates, allowing for more immediate and less formal communication.

Email continues to be a staple for more formal and detailed communication. However, email communication should be clear and concise to avoid misinterpretation and information overload. Shared collaborative tools like Google Workspace or Microsoft 365 enable teams to work together on documents, spreadsheets, and presentations, ensuring everyone is on the same page.

Balancing synchronous and asynchronous communication methods is crucial in remote teams, especially when working across different time zones. Synchronous communication, such as video calls or real-time chat, is important for immediate collaboration and building relationships. Asynchronous communication, like emails and shared documents, provides flexibility, allowing team members to contribute at a time that suits them best. It's important to establish guidelines on when to use each type of communication, respecting each team member's time and workload.

Regular team meetings and one-on-one check-ins are also important practices. They provide opportunities for updates, feedback, and addressing any issues or concerns. These meetings should be structured and purposeful to maximize efficiency and respect everyone's time.

Adapting performance management processes for remote teams is essential to ensure that employees remain productive, motivated, and aligned with organizational goals. In a remote setting, traditional methods of performance evaluation, which often rely heavily on physical presence and observation, need to be rethought and revised.

One of the key elements of effective performance management in remote settings is setting clear goals and expectations. Remote workers benefit from having specific, measurable, achievable, relevant, and time-bound (SMART) goals. These objectives provide clarity and direction, helping remote employees understand what is expected of them and how their work contributes to the broader goals of the organization.

Feedback mechanisms are also crucial in a remote work environment. Regular check-ins, whether weekly or bi-weekly, can provide opportunities for managers and employees to discuss progress, address challenges, and adjust goals as necessary. These sessions should be a two-way street, allowing employees to voice their concerns and feedback about their work environment and tasks.

Technology plays a significant role in performance management for remote teams. Various digital tools and software can be used to track and evaluate performance. Project management tools like Asana or Trello can help managers monitor progress on specific tasks and projects. Time-tracking software can offer insights into how employees are managing their time, while also respecting their privacy and autonomy.

Performance evaluations in a remote setting should also consider the quality of work and the impact on team and organizational objectives, rather than just focusing on the quantity of work done or hours logged. This approach acknowledges the unique aspects of remote work, such as flexible schedules and the need for self-motivation and discipline.

Another important aspect is recognizing and rewarding achievements. In a remote setting, where employees may feel disconnected, acknowledging their hard work and contributions can significantly boost morale and motivation. This can be done through virtual recognition, bonuses, promotions, or other forms of rewards. It's important to provide opportunities for professional development and growth. Remote employees should have access to training programs, webinars, and other resources to help them advance their skills and careers.

Performance management in a remote setting requires clear goal-setting, regular and constructive feedback, the use of technology to track progress, a focus on the quality and impact of work, recognition of achievements, and opportunities for professional growth. By adapting these practices to suit remote environments, organizations can ensure effective performance management that supports their employees and aligns with their objectives.

Promoting work-life balance in remote teams is essential, as the lines between professional and personal life can often blur in a home working environment, leading to challenges such as overworking and burnout. Addressing these challenges requires deliberate strategies and practices that help employees establish and maintain healthy boundaries.

One significant challenge in remote work is the tendency to work longer hours, which can quickly lead to burnout. Employers can help manage this by setting clear expectations about work hours and respecting employees' time off. Encouraging employees to stick to a regular work schedule and discouraging after-hours communication unless it's urgent can reinforce these boundaries.

Encouraging employees to create a dedicated workspace in their home can also help in maintaining work-life balance. A separate workspace can create a physical boundary between work and personal life, helping employees switch off from work mode once the workday is over.

Promoting regular breaks throughout the day is another effective strategy. Encouraging employees to take short, regular breaks away from their workstations can prevent fatigue and boost productivity. Employers can foster this culture by modeling this behavior themselves and even organizing virtual coffee breaks or short group activities. Managers play a crucial role in promoting work-life balance. They should be trained to recognize the signs of burnout and stress in their team members. Regular check-ins can provide a platform for employees to discuss any challenges they are facing, including issues related to work-life balance.

Organizations can also provide resources and support for mental health and well-being. This could include access to counseling services, workshops on stress management, or subscriptions to mindfulness and wellness apps. Encouraging physical activity and wellness is also beneficial. Employers can offer virtual fitness classes, wellness challenges, or stipends for gym memberships to encourage a healthy lifestyle, which is crucial for maintaining a good work-life balance. Promoting a culture that values work-life balance is key. This can be done through company policies, leadership examples, and regular communication that emphasizes the organization's commitment to the well-being of its employees.

Promoting work-life balance in remote teams requires setting clear boundaries, providing support for mental and physical health, and fostering a culture that values and respects the personal time and well-being of employees. By implementing these strategies, organizations can help their remote teams maintain a healthy balance between their professional and personal lives.

Building and maintaining a strong work culture in a remote team is pivotal for ensuring team cohesion, employee satisfaction, and overall productivity. The lack of a physical office environment in remote settings poses unique challenges in instilling and upholding company values and culture. However, with thoughtful strategies and practices, it's possible to foster a vibrant and unified work culture remotely.

Firstly, clear and consistent communication of company values is essential. This can be achieved through regular virtual meetings, company-wide newsletters, and digital platforms where the company's mission, vision, and values are prominently displayed and discussed. Leaders should consistently embody and reinforce these values in their interactions and decision-making processes. Creating opportunities for regular interaction and team bonding is crucial in a remote setting. Virtual team-building activities, social hours, and informal catch-up sessions can help strengthen relationships and foster a sense of belonging among team members. These activities should be inclusive and consider the different time zones, cultures, and personal commitments of team members.

Recognition and celebration of achievements play a significant role in maintaining a positive work culture. Acknowledging individual and team successes, whether through virtual shout-outs, reward programs, or celebratory meetings, can boost morale and reinforce a culture of appreciation and recognition. Encouraging open and transparent communication is another best practice. Creating channels where employees can share ideas, give feedback, and voice concerns without fear of retribution helps in building trust and a sense of community. Regular surveys, open forums, and suggestion boxes can be effective tools for this purpose.

Training and development opportunities are also integral to a strong work culture. Providing access to online learning resources, virtual workshops, and webinars can help employees grow and develop within the company, reinforcing a culture of continuous learning and development.

Fostering a sense of inclusivity and diversity is equally important. This involves ensuring that all team members, regardless of their location, feel valued and included. Inclusive practices might include diverse hiring policies, celebrating different cultural events, and ensuring that all voices are heard in meetings and decision-making processes. Leadership plays a crucial role in shaping the work culture in a remote team. Leaders who are approachable, empathetic, and responsive to the needs of their team set a positive example and create an environment where employees feel supported and valued.

Building and maintaining a strong work culture in a remote team requires clear communication of company values, regular interaction and team bonding, recognition of achievements, open communication, opportunities for growth and development, inclusivity, and strong leadership. By embracing these practices, organizations can foster a cohesive and vibrant remote work culture that aligns with their core values and objectives. As remote team management becomes increasingly prevalent in the modern workplace, anticipating and preparing for future trends and challenges is crucial for organizations. The landscape of remote work is continually evolving, influenced by technological advancements, changing employee expectations, and broader socio-economic factors. Leaders in this environment must embrace flexibility and continuous learning to navigate these changes effectively.

One of the key future trends in remote team management is the growing need for digital proficiency. As new tools and technologies emerge, leaders and their teams must be adept at leveraging these for efficient collaboration and productivity. This may involve staying updated with the latest communication and project management tools, cybersecurity practices, and emerging technologies like AI and machine learning that could impact work processes.

Another challenge is managing a diverse and globally dispersed workforce. As remote work breaks down geographical barriers, teams are becoming more culturally diverse. Leaders must be equipped to handle the nuances of cross-cultural communication and inclusive leadership, ensuring that all team members feel valued and understood regardless of their background.
The mental health and well-being of remote employees will continue to be a critical focus. Future remote team management will need to address challenges related to isolation, burnout, and work-life balance in increasingly innovative ways. This could

involve implementing more holistic wellness programs, flexible working policies, and regular check-ins focused on well-being.

Adapting to changing employee expectations and workstyles is another area of focus. The future workforce may demand greater flexibility, autonomy, and opportunities for personal and professional growth. Leaders must be prepared to offer varied and dynamic working arrangements and foster a culture of trust and accountability. The importance of flexibility and continuous learning in leadership cannot be overstated. Future remote work environments will require leaders to be adaptable, open to feedback, and willing to revise strategies and approaches as necessary. This involves being open to new ideas, willing to experiment with different management styles, and continually seeking to enhance their skills and knowledge.

Preparing for future challenges in remote team management involves staying abreast of technological trends, embracing cultural diversity, prioritizing employee well-being, adapting to changing workstyles, and fostering a culture of flexibility and continuous learning. By anticipating these trends and challenges, leaders can ensure that their remote teams remain productive, engaged, and well-prepared for the future of work.

Effective remote team management hinges on clear and consistent communication. Leaders need to ensure that team objectives, expectations, and progress are transparently conveyed to foster a sense of clarity and direction. Regular check-ins and open lines of communication are crucial to maintaining team alignment and addressing any issues promptly.

The importance of building and maintaining a strong team culture, even in a remote setting, cannot be understated. This involves not just integrating company values into everyday interactions but also creating opportunities for team bonding and recognition of achievements. Celebrating successes, acknowledging individual contributions, and providing opportunities for informal interactions help in creating a cohesive and motivated team.

Adapting performance management processes for remote settings is another key insight. Setting clear goals, utilizing technology for tracking performance, and offering regular feedback are essential practices. Emphasizing outcomes rather than hours worked, and focusing on the quality of work, aligns with the nature of remote work.

Promoting work-life balance is vital in remote settings. Encouraging employees to establish a clear distinction between work and personal time, advocating for regular breaks, and respecting employees' time outside of work hours are practices that help prevent burnout and maintain employee well-being.

The role of IT support and the right technological tools is pivotal in remote team management. Ensuring that team members have the necessary resources, training, and support to effectively use technology is fundamental to a productive remote work environment. Leadership in remote teams requires a blend of flexibility, empathy, and continuous learning. Being adaptable to changing circumstances, understanding the unique challenges faced by remote employees, and continually updating skills and knowledge are key to effective remote team management.

As we transition to the next chapter, we will dive into real-world case studies in hybrid workplaces. These case studies will offer practical insights into how different organizations have successfully navigated the challenges and leveraged the opportunities presented by hybrid work models. We'll explore diverse scenarios, learning from the experiences and strategies of these organizations, providing a richer understanding of the practical application of the concepts discussed in managing remote teams.

# Chapter 8: Case Studies in Hybrid Workplaces

The purpose of examining case studies is multifold. Firstly, they offer tangible examples of how organizations across different industries have navigated the transition to hybrid work. This includes challenges they faced, solutions they implemented, and the outcomes of these changes. These real-world examples serve as a rich source of learning, offering practical insights that can be applied to other organizations considering or currently managing hybrid work models.

Each case study highlights diverse applications of hybrid work models, showcasing how different organizations have tailored these models to suit their specific needs, culture, and operational demands. This diversity illustrates the flexibility of hybrid work models and their applicability across various sectors and organizational sizes. Furthermore, these case studies provide valuable lessons on strategies for effective communication, maintaining company culture, ensuring productivity, and managing employee well-being in a hybrid setting. They offer a glimpse into the innovative practices and tools that organizations have adopted to overcome the challenges associated with hybrid work.

By setting the stage with these case studies, we aim to provide a comprehensive understanding of the varied and dynamic nature of hybrid workplaces. The insights gleaned from these examples will not only demonstrate the potential benefits and challenges of hybrid work models but also highlight the importance of adaptability, strategic planning, and ongoing evaluation in their successful implementation.

As we proceed through the chapter, these case studies will serve as a guide and inspiration, offering a practical perspective on the realities of hybrid work environments and how they can be effectively managed and optimized for success.

The successful implementation of hybrid work models across various sectors highlights the adaptability and innovation of organizations in response to changing work dynamics. Here, we profile a range of organizations from different sectors, including tech, finance, healthcare, and education, detailing their journey in adopting hybrid models – the initial challenges they faced, the strategies they employed, and the outcomes they achieved.

In the tech sector, a prominent software company faced the challenge of transitioning its workforce to a hybrid model while maintaining its collaborative and innovative culture. The initial challenge was ensuring all employees had access to necessary technology and tools for effective remote work. Their strategy included investing in cloud-based collaborative tools and training sessions to familiarize employees with remote working best practices. The outcome was a successful transition, with employees reporting higher job satisfaction and productivity, and the company maintaining its pace of innovation.

A global financial institution had to navigate the complexities of handling sensitive data and client interactions in a hybrid setup. Their initial challenge was ensuring data security and regulatory compliance. The organization implemented robust cybersecurity measures, including secure VPNs and multi-factor authentication, and established clear guidelines on handling sensitive information in remote settings. The result was a seamless transition to hybrid work, with no compromise on data security and an increase in employee flexibility.

In healthcare, a hospital network adopted a hybrid model for its administrative and support staff while ensuring uninterrupted patient care. The challenge was maintaining effective communication between remote and on-site staff and ensuring continuity of administrative functions. They introduced a unified communication platform and regular virtual meetings to ensure alignment. The outcome was a successful hybrid model that reduced overhead costs and allowed administrative staff greater work flexibility without affecting patient care.

An educational institution, facing the sudden need to shift to remote learning, adopted a hybrid model for both teaching and administrative staff. The initial challenge was the lack of experience with remote teaching tools and methodologies. The institution provided extensive training for faculty in online teaching platforms and digital pedagogy. The transition led to a successful hybrid learning environment, with teachers adept at both in-person and online teaching methods.

These diverse sector representations show that while the challenges in implementing hybrid models vary across industries, the key to success often lies in strategic planning, investing in the right technology, and ensuring employee training and well-being. These case studies demonstrate the potential of hybrid work models to enhance flexibility, productivity, and employee satisfaction across different work environments. In hybrid work, innovation and creativity are key drivers that enable organizations to tailor their work models to meet specific needs and challenges. By exploring case studies that highlight unique approaches to hybrid work, we can glean insights into how different organizations have creatively adapted to this new work paradigm.

One notable example is a technology startup that redefined its workspace by transforming its office into a collaborative hub. Instead of mandating regular office attendance, the company encouraged employees to use the office space primarily for team meetings, brainstorming sessions, and collaborative projects, while routine tasks were handled remotely. This approach led to a significant increase in creative collaboration and team bonding, without compromising individual flexibility.

Another innovative approach was adopted by a marketing agency that implemented a 'results-only work environment' (ROWE). In this model, employees had complete autonomy over their work location and hours, as long as they met predefined performance metrics and project deadlines. This focus on results rather than hours spent working led to improved productivity and employee satisfaction, as team members were able to work in ways that best suited their personal productivity rhythms.

A multinational corporation introduced a hybrid rotational system where different departments worked on-site on designated days of the week. This system was designed to ensure that employees could benefit from in-person interactions and collaboration, while also enjoying the flexibility of remote work. Additionally, the company invested in state-of-the-art video conferencing facilities to ensure seamless communication between remote and on-site employees.

In the education sector, a university pioneered a hybrid teaching model that combined in-person and online learning. Lectures were delivered live with remote students participating virtually, and supplementary materials were provided through an online platform. This model not only catered to the diverse needs of students but also prepared them for a future where digital collaboration is commonplace.

These examples showcase how different organizations have tailored their hybrid work models to suit their unique needs and objectives. Creative solutions to common hybrid work challenges, such as maintaining team cohesion, ensuring productivity, and fostering a collaborative culture, are at the heart of these innovative approaches. These case studies serve as inspiration for other organizations navigating the hybrid work landscape, demonstrating that with a bit of creativity and strategic planning, the challenges of hybrid work can be transformed into opportunities for growth and innovation.

The transition to hybrid work models often presents a set of common hurdles that organizations must navigate. Identifying these challenges and discussing the strategies and solutions employed to overcome them provides valuable insights for any organization embarking on this journey. One common challenge is resistance to change, both from management and staff. Many organizations have long-established cultures and practices centered around in-office work, and shifting to a hybrid model can be met with skepticism. To overcome this, successful organizations often employ transparent communication strategies, explaining the benefits of hybrid work and addressing concerns. They also involve employees in the planning process, making the transition a collaborative effort.

Another hurdle is ensuring effective communication and collaboration among team members who are working both remotely and on-site. The lack of face-to-face interaction can lead to miscommunications or feelings of isolation. To combat this, many organizations invest in advanced communication technologies like video conferencing tools and collaborative software platforms. They also establish regular check-ins and virtual meetings to maintain team cohesion and ensure everyone stays informed.

Ensuring productivity and accountability in a remote environment is another challenge. Without the physical oversight found in traditional office settings, managers may struggle to monitor and evaluate employee performance effectively. Organizations have tackled this by setting clear goals and expectations, using project management tools to track progress, and focusing on output rather than hours worked. Maintaining company culture and employee engagement in a hybrid setting can also be challenging. Organizations have found success by creating virtual spaces for social interaction, celebrating achievements, and ensuring that remote employees feel as much a part of the team as those who are in the office.

Addressing the technical aspects of a hybrid model is another common challenge. This includes providing employees with the necessary hardware and software to work efficiently from home and ensuring robust cybersecurity measures are in place. Offering technical support and training for remote working tools is also crucial. Organizations often face logistical challenges in configuring physical office spaces to accommodate a hybrid model. This can involve redesigning office layouts to support collaborative work when employees are on-site and ensuring health and safety measures are in place.

Overcoming the initial challenges of transitioning to hybrid work models involves a combination of strategic planning, investment in technology, fostering open communication, and adapting management and cultural practices. By employing these strategies, organizations can effectively navigate the early hurdles of implementing a hybrid work model.

The long-term sustainability of hybrid work models hinges on the ability of organizations to continuously adapt and evolve these models in response to changing circumstances, technological advancements, and employee feedback. This adaptive approach ensures that the hybrid model remains effective, relevant, and beneficial over time.

Many organizations have realized that the initial transition to a hybrid model is just the beginning. For long-term sustainability, they continuously assess and refine their approach. This involves regular feedback loops with employees to understand their experiences, challenges, and needs in the hybrid setup. Surveys, focus groups, and open forums can be instrumental in gathering this feedback, which can then inform adjustments and improvements to the model.

Adapting to changing circumstances is another key aspect of ensuring the sustainability of hybrid models. This could involve flexing the balance between remote and in-office work in response to external factors such as public health guidelines, or internal factors like project demands or team dynamics. Organizations that remain flexible and responsive to these changing needs are better positioned to sustain their hybrid models effectively.

Technological advancements also play a significant role in the long-term sustainability of hybrid work. As new tools and platforms emerge, organizations must stay abreast of these developments and integrate them into their hybrid work infrastructure. This ensures that employees have access to the best tools for communication, collaboration, and productivity.

Another important aspect is the ongoing training and support for employees. As hybrid work models evolve, so do the skills and competencies required to work effectively in them. Providing regular training on new technologies, communication best practices, and time management can help employees adapt to the evolving demands of hybrid work. Many organizations are finding that sustaining a hybrid model requires a cultural shift that embraces flexibility, autonomy, and trust. Cultivating a culture that supports these values can help ensure that employees feel supported and engaged in the hybrid model over the long term. The physical workspace itself may need to evolve. Organizations are rethinking their office designs to make them more conducive to the needs of a hybrid workforce, such as creating more collaborative spaces and ensuring that on-site facilities support a productive work environment.

The long-term sustainability of hybrid models depends on an organization's ability to continuously evolve and adapt. This involves regularly seeking and responding to employee feedback, staying flexible to changing needs, leveraging technological advancements, providing ongoing training and support, fostering a supportive culture, and adapting the physical workspace as needed. By embracing these practices, organizations can ensure that their hybrid work models remain effective and beneficial in the long run.

The case studies presented in this chapter offer a wealth of insights and lessons on the implementation and management of hybrid work models. Drawing from these real-world examples, we can summarize a set of best practices and recommendations that are critical for the successful adoption of hybrid workplace models.

1. Flexibility and Adaptability: A recurring theme across the case studies is the importance of flexibility in both policy and practice. Successful hybrid models are those that can adapt to changing circumstances and individual employee needs. This

includes allowing for variations in work hours, locations, and adapting strategies as required.

2. Effective Communication: Clear, consistent, and open communication is essential in hybrid workplaces. Regular check-ins, all-hands meetings, and transparent communication channels help in keeping remote and on-site team members aligned and informed.

3. Investment in Technology: The right technological infrastructure is fundamental to the success of hybrid models. This involves not only providing the necessary tools for remote work but also ensuring that these tools are reliable, secure, and easy to use.

4. Employee Engagement and Inclusion: Actively working to maintain team cohesion and a sense of belonging is crucial, especially for remote employees who might feel disconnected. Virtual team-building activities, informal catch-ups, and inclusive practices help in fostering a strong team culture.

5. Training and Support: Providing employees with training on remote work tools and best practices is vital. Additionally, offering ongoing support, especially in terms of IT and mental health resources, is critical for the well-being and productivity of the team.

6. Focus on Output, Not Hours: Shifting the focus from hours worked to the quality and impact of work encourages productivity and job satisfaction. This approach respects the autonomy of employees and aligns with the flexible nature of hybrid work.

7. Regular Feedback and Iteration: Continuous feedback from employees is invaluable for refining hybrid work models. Regular surveys, feedback sessions, and a willingness to iterate policies based on this feedback are key to evolving and sustaining effective hybrid models.

8. Leadership and Management Training: Equipping leaders and managers with the skills to manage remote teams effectively is essential. This includes training in remote team leadership, empathy, and digital communication.

9. Maintaining Security and Compliance: Ensuring data security and regulatory compliance, especially in a dispersed work environment, is a priority. Regular reviews of security protocols and compliance training for staff are necessary measures.

10. Work-Life Balance: Encouraging a healthy work-life balance is important to prevent burnout. This includes respecting boundaries, encouraging regular breaks, and being mindful of employees' personal time.

These insights and best practices drawn from the case studies provide a roadmap for organizations looking to implement or enhance their hybrid work models. The key to success lies in being adaptable, employee-centric, and technologically equipped, coupled with strong leadership and a focus on communication and culture.

The shift to hybrid work models has profound implications for organizational culture and employee well-being. As these models blend remote and in-office work, they inherently alter the dynamics of how employees interact, collaborate, and connect with the organization. Understanding these effects and how organizations have navigated them provides valuable insights into the potential of hybrid models to foster positive work environments.

One significant effect of hybrid models is their impact on organizational culture. Culture in a workplace is traditionally built through shared experiences and interactions within a physical office space. In a hybrid setting, maintaining this sense of community and shared purpose requires deliberate effort. Organizations successful in this transition have often relied on regular virtual team-building activities, consistent and transparent communication from leadership, and digital platforms that facilitate informal interactions among employees. These efforts help maintain a sense of cohesion and belonging, even when face-to-face interactions are limited.

Another key aspect is reshaping the culture to fit the hybrid model. This often involves emphasizing values such as flexibility, autonomy, trust, and results-oriented performance. By fostering a culture that aligns with these values, organizations can ensure that their culture supports, rather than conflicts with, the hybrid model. For example, encouraging flexibility and autonomy can help employees feel empowered in managing their work and personal responsibilities, leading to higher job satisfaction and productivity.

Employee well-being in hybrid models is another crucial consideration. The flexibility of hybrid work can significantly contribute to a better work-life balance, reducing stress and improving overall well-being. However, the risk of isolation and burnout, particularly for those who predominantly work remotely, requires careful management. Organizations have addressed this by providing resources for mental health, such as access to counseling services, wellness programs, and regular check-ins focused on well-being.

Effective communication and support from managers and team leaders play a vital role in employee well-being. Ensuring that remote employees feel equally seen, heard, and valued as their in-office counterparts is crucial for their mental and emotional well-being. The impact of hybrid models on organizational culture and employee well-being is multifaceted. Maintaining or reshaping culture in a hybrid setting involves fostering values that support flexible working, leveraging technology to maintain team cohesion, and prioritizing employee well-being. By addressing these aspects thoughtfully, organizations can create a hybrid work environment that not only preserves but potentially enhances their culture and the overall well-being of their employees.

As organizations navigate the evolving landscape of hybrid work, preparing for future changes and potential challenges is crucial. The case studies reveal that successful organizations are those that embrace innovation and adaptability, continuously improving their hybrid work models in response to new developments and insights.

One key area of focus is the anticipation of technological advancements. As new tools and platforms emerge, organizations must be ready to integrate them into their existing infrastructure to enhance collaboration and productivity. This requires staying abreast of tech trends and being open to experimenting with new solutions that could improve the hybrid work experience. Another aspect is the continuous collection and analysis of feedback from employees. Regular surveys, feedback sessions, and open channels of communication help organizations gauge the effectiveness of their hybrid models and identify areas for improvement. This feedback is invaluable in making iterative adjustments to work policies, practices, and environments to better suit the evolving needs of the workforce.

Organizational flexibility is also paramount in preparing for future adaptations. This includes being ready to adjust the balance between remote and in-office work as circumstances change, such as shifts in public health guidelines, employee preferences, or business needs. A flexible approach allows organizations to respond swiftly and effectively to external and internal changes. Innovation in management and leadership practices is another critical area for future adaptations. As hybrid work models continue to evolve, so too must the strategies for leading and managing remote teams. This could involve further training for managers in remote leadership, investing in tools that facilitate remote team management, and developing new metrics for evaluating employee performance in a hybrid setup.

Organizations are recognizing the importance of maintaining a strong company culture and employee engagement in a hybrid setting. This may involve innovative approaches to team building, collaboration, and ensuring that remote employees feel as connected and involved as their in-office counterparts.

Preparing for future adaptations in hybrid work models requires a commitment to innovation, flexibility, and continuous improvement. By staying attuned to technological developments, actively seeking employee feedback, remaining adaptable to changing circumstances, and continuously innovating in management practices, organizations can ensure their hybrid work models remain effective, efficient, and beneficial for all stakeholders in the long term.

As we conclude our exploration of the case studies in hybrid workplaces, it's clear that these real-world examples provide a rich and nuanced understanding of how organizations are navigating the shift to hybrid work models. These case studies are significant as they offer practical insights and lessons that can be applied across various industries and organizational sizes.

From the technology startups to multinational corporations, the diverse range of organizations profiled demonstrates that hybrid work models are not a one-size-fits-all solution. Instead, they require customization and adaptation to fit specific organizational contexts and cultures. The case studies reveal the importance of flexibility, communication, technology, and leadership in making hybrid work successful.

A key takeaway from these case studies is the critical role of adaptability in today's evolving work culture. The ability to adapt to changing circumstances, employee needs, and technological advancements is a defining characteristic of organizations that have successfully implemented hybrid models. This adaptability is not just a response to the challenges posed by hybrid work but is also a proactive approach to leveraging its opportunities.

Another significant insight is the emphasis on maintaining and reshaping organizational culture in a hybrid environment. The case studies show that despite the physical separation of team members, it's possible to foster a strong and cohesive culture through shared values, regular communication, and inclusive practices. This requires a conscious effort from leadership and a commitment to ensuring that all employees, regardless of their location, feel connected and engaged.

The importance of continuous learning and innovation also emerges as a vital theme. As work environments continue to evolve, organizations must remain open to learning and experimenting with new tools, strategies, and management practices. This continuous evolution is essential for staying relevant and competitive in a rapidly changing work landscape.

The case studies in hybrid workplaces provide invaluable insights into the complexities and potential of hybrid work models. They underscore the need for flexibility, innovation, and a focus on culture and communication. As organizations around the world continue to navigate the shift to hybrid work, the lessons from these case studies offer guidance and inspiration, highlighting the possibilities for creating more dynamic, inclusive, and effective work environments.

# Part 3: Integrating Generative AI and Hybrid Work Models

In Part 3 of "The Future of Work Now," we venture into the compelling intersection of generative AI and hybrid work models, weaving together the insights gathered from the initial sections of the book. This part is dedicated to understanding how the innovative capabilities of generative AI can be harmoniously integrated into the flexible, often fluid, realms of hybrid work environments. Our aim here is to create a mosaic of strategies and insights that can guide organizations in merging the potential of AI with the adaptability of hybrid workplaces.

We start by exploring how generative AI can blend into and enhance hybrid work cultures in Chapter 9. This chapter delves into the practical aspects of using AI to maintain productivity while adding to the flexibility that defines hybrid work. We examine the role of AI in ensuring effective communication and collaboration across geographically dispersed teams and how AI tools can be customized to meet the unique demands of hybrid work settings.

In Chapter 10, the focus shifts to skill development and training in an environment where AI and hybrid work coexist. Recognizing the dual needs for AI literacy and remote working competencies, this chapter outlines strategies to upskill the workforce, ensuring they are equipped to navigate an AI-integrated, hybrid work landscape. Leadership development also takes center stage, emphasizing the cultivation of leaders proficient in managing hybrid teams and adept in leveraging AI for insightful decision-making.

Ethical management forms the core of Chapter 11, where we tackle the complex ethical considerations arising at the intersection of AI and hybrid work. This includes developing comprehensive ethical frameworks to address issues like data privacy and surveillance and ensuring fairness and inclusivity in both remote and in-office settings. The chapter underscores the importance of ethical vigilance in an AI-driven hybrid work environment.

Chapter 12 brings to life the theoretical concepts discussed previously through a series of case studies. These real-world examples showcase organizations that have successfully integrated generative AI into their hybrid work models. By analyzing these cases, we draw out actionable insights and best practices, offering a practical blueprint for organizations looking to embark on a similar journey.

In this concluding part of the book, we aim to provide a holistic view of how generative AI and hybrid work models can not only coexist but actively complement and enhance each other, paving the way for a more dynamic, efficient, and inclusive future of work.

# Chapter 9: Blending AI with Hybrid Work Cultures

We continue our exploration into the burgeoning intersection of generative AI and hybrid work models. This integration represents a fusion of technological innovation with new ways of working, promising to reshape the landscape of the modern workplace significantly. This chapter aims to provide an overview of the synergy between these two domains and set the stage for understanding how AI can be integrated effectively in diverse work environments.

The integration of AI in hybrid work cultures is not just about the implementation of new technologies but also about harmonizing these technologies with the human aspects of work. AI offers a range of possibilities to enhance efficiency, productivity, and creativity in hybrid workplaces. From automating routine tasks to providing advanced analytics and facilitating better decision-making, AI has the potential to augment the capabilities of human workers significantly.

However, this integration also brings challenges and considerations, particularly in terms of maintaining a balance between technological efficiency and human-centric work practices. Issues such as workforce training, ethical use of AI, and the potential impact on employment and job roles are critical considerations in this integration.

Understanding the integration of AI in hybrid work environments also involves exploring its application across various sectors and job functions. Whether it's in enhancing communication and collaboration across distributed teams, optimizing workflow management in a flexible work setting, or offering personalized learning and development opportunities for employees, AI's role is multifaceted.

In this chapter, we delve into various case studies and examples that demonstrate how different organizations are navigating the integration of AI into their hybrid work cultures. These examples will shed light on the practical aspects of this integration, highlighting innovative uses of AI, strategies for overcoming challenges, and the tangible benefits that AI can bring to hybrid work settings.

The overarching theme of this chapter is the exploration of how AI and hybrid work models can complement and enhance each other, leading to work environments that are not only more efficient and productive but also more adaptable and human-centric. As we navigate through this chapter, the aim is to provide a comprehensive understanding of how AI can be seamlessly and ethically integrated into hybrid workplaces, contributing to the evolution of work culture in the digital age. The integration of generative AI into hybrid work models offers a unique opportunity to enhance the inherent flexibility of these arrangements while maintaining or even improving productivity. This harmonization of technology with flexibility is key to the successful adoption of AI in hybrid workplaces.

Generative AI, with its ability to automate complex tasks, analyze large datasets, and generate creative solutions, can be a powerful tool in supporting the flexible nature of hybrid work. For instance, AI-driven tools can automate routine administrative tasks, freeing up employees to focus on more strategic and creative work that can be done flexibly in terms of time and location.

AI can also play a crucial role in project management and workflow optimization in hybrid settings. By analyzing work patterns and project timelines, AI systems can optimize schedules and allocate resources efficiently, accommodating the varying schedules and locations of team members. This ensures that productivity is maintained even when team members are working asynchronously or from different locations.

Moreover, AI-driven communication and collaboration tools can enhance the flexibility of hybrid work models. These tools can provide real-time translation and transcription services, making it easier for globally dispersed teams to collaborate. AI can also personalize information feeds and notifications, ensuring that team members receive relevant updates without being overwhelmed, thus aiding in maintaining focus and efficiency.

AI can offer advanced analytics and insights that help managers track progress and identify areas for improvement. Predictive analytics can foresee potential bottlenecks or delays in projects, allowing teams to proactively address issues before they impact productivity.

Integrating AI into hybrid work models also requires careful consideration of potential challenges. Ensuring that AI tools are user-friendly and accessible to all employees, regardless of their technical expertise, is vital. Additionally, training and support are crucial in helping employees adapt to AI-driven tools and processes, ensuring they feel confident and capable in this enhanced work environment. Harmonizing generative AI with the flexibility of hybrid work models involves leveraging AI to automate routine tasks, optimize workflows, enhance communication, and provide valuable insights, all while ensuring ease of use and accessibility. By doing so, organizations can harness the full potential of AI to support flexible work arrangements, ultimately leading to improved productivity and a more dynamic, responsive work environment.

The integration of AI in facilitating communication and enhancing collaboration is a critical component in hybrid work environments, especially for distributed teams. AI tools can significantly streamline interactions and foster a collaborative spirit, even when team members are physically apart. AI-driven communication tools are revolutionizing how teams interact. For instance, AI-powered chatbots and virtual assistants can help manage and prioritize communications, schedule meetings, and provide timely reminders. AI can also enhance video conferencing tools, offering features like real-time transcription, translation, and sentiment analysis, making digital meetings more accessible and efficient, especially for teams spread across different linguistic and cultural backgrounds.

In terms of collaboration, AI is playing a transformative role. AI-driven project management tools can predict project timelines, allocate resources optimally, and identify potential risks by analyzing historical data. This proactive approach aids in keeping projects on track and teams aligned with their goals. Additionally, AI can assist in document collaboration by suggesting edits, providing contextually relevant information, and even drafting content in some cases.

Examples of AI-driven collaboration tools include platforms that intelligently categorize and prioritize emails and work tasks, collaboration platforms that suggest relevant documents or experts based on the context of the project, and creative tools that offer design or content suggestions based on current trends and past preferences. Implementing AI for communication and collaboration in a hybrid setup is not without its challenges. One primary concern is ensuring the accessibility and usability of these AI tools for all team members, regardless of their technical proficiency. It's crucial that these tools are intuitive and require minimal training to use effectively. Another challenge is data privacy and security. As AI tools often require access to sensitive company and employee data to function optimally, ensuring that this data is handled securely and in compliance with privacy regulations is paramount. There is also the challenge of avoiding over-reliance on AI, which might lead to a reduction in personal interactions that are crucial for team bonding and creativity. Balancing AI-driven efficiency with the human elements of collaboration is essential.

To address these challenges, organizations need to adopt a strategic approach to implementing AI tools. This includes thorough vetting of tools for security and compliance, providing comprehensive training and support to employees, and fostering a culture that values both technological efficiency and personal interactions.

AI has the potential to significantly enhance communication and collaboration in hybrid work environments. By choosing the right tools, addressing challenges related to usability, security, and maintaining the human touch, organizations can leverage AI to foster a more connected, productive, and collaborative workforce.

Customizing AI tools to suit the unique needs of hybrid workplaces is a critical step in ensuring these technologies effectively support both remote and office work settings. Tailoring AI applications involves understanding the specific challenges and requirements of hybrid environments and adapting the technology to meet these needs. One key strategy is identifying the specific pain points and objectives within a hybrid work model. For example, if the main challenge is maintaining team cohesion, AI tools that facilitate team interaction and collaboration could be prioritized. On the other hand, if the focus is on productivity and workflow management, AI applications that automate routine tasks and optimize project management could be more beneficial.

Analyzing the effectiveness of AI tools in both remote and office settings is crucial. AI tools need to provide value in diverse work environments. For instance, AI-driven communication tools should be as effective in facilitating virtual meetings as they are in enhancing in-person interactions with digital aids. Similarly, project management AI should seamlessly integrate tasks and updates across remote and in-office employees.

Case studies of organizations that have successfully adapted AI tools for their hybrid environments offer valuable insights. For instance, a tech company might use AI-driven analytics tools to monitor and analyze workflow patterns, identifying bottlenecks that occur in remote work settings and using these insights to improve processes. Another example could be a marketing firm using AI-powered content creation tools, enabling team members to collaboratively design and edit materials, regardless of their physical location.

Another important aspect is customization based on user feedback. Regularly soliciting feedback from employees on the effectiveness and usability of AI tools can provide insights into how these tools can be better tailored to meet the needs of a hybrid workforce. Continuous iteration based on this feedback can significantly enhance the utility of AI applications in a hybrid setting.

Training and support are also crucial for effective customization. Employees should be provided with adequate training to use AI tools effectively. This includes not only technical training but also guidance on how to integrate these tools into their daily work processes to maximize benefits.

Customizing AI tools for hybrid environments involves identifying specific workplace needs, ensuring the effectiveness of these tools across different work settings, learning from successful case studies, incorporating user feedback, and providing comprehensive training and support. By adopting these strategies, organizations can tailor AI applications to enhance their hybrid work models effectively, leading to increased efficiency, productivity, and employee satisfaction.

Training and adaptation are crucial for successful AI integration in hybrid work models, especially considering the diverse technological proficiency among team members. Adequate training ensures that all employees can effectively utilize AI tools, thereby maximizing the benefits these technologies bring to the hybrid work environment.

Addressing the training needs for employees involves several key steps:

1. Assessment of Skill Levels: Before implementing training programs, it's important to assess the current AI literacy and technology skill levels of the workforce. This assessment helps in tailoring the training to meet the varying needs of different team members.

2. Customized Training Programs: Based on the skill assessment, organizations should develop customized training programs. These programs might range from basic AI and technology orientation for beginners to more advanced training for tech-savvy employees. Ensuring that training is relevant and applicable to employees' specific roles and functions is crucial.

3. Interactive and Engaging Learning Methods: Incorporating a mix of training methods, such as workshops, webinars, interactive e-learning modules, and hands-on practice sessions can cater to different learning styles. Gamification and real-life scenarios can also make the learning process more engaging and effective.

4. Continuous Learning and Support: AI and technology landscapes are constantly evolving. Providing ongoing learning opportunities and resources, such as access to online courses, tech talks, and forums, can help employees stay updated with the latest advancements.

5. Mentorship and Peer Learning: Establishing a mentorship program or peer learning groups where more technologically adept employees guide others can be an effective way of fostering a culture of learning and collaboration.

6. Encouraging Experimentation: Creating an environment where employees feel safe to experiment with AI tools and learn from their experiences can foster quicker adaptation. Encouraging exploration and not penalizing mistakes during the learning process is essential.

7. Feedback Mechanisms: Implementing feedback channels where employees can express their concerns, challenges, and suggestions regarding AI tools and training can help organizations refine their approach and address any ongoing issues.

8. Leadership Involvement and Support: Leadership support is key to successful AI integration. Leaders should actively endorse and participate in training programs to demonstrate the organization's commitment to AI adoption.

9. Communication of Benefits: Clearly communicating the benefits of AI integration, such as increased efficiency, easier task management, and enhanced decision-making, can motivate employees to embrace the change.

10. Accessibility Considerations: Ensuring that training and AI tools are accessible to all employees, including those with disabilities, is vital for inclusive adoption.

Facilitating the smooth adoption of AI technologies in a hybrid work environment requires a comprehensive and continuous training approach, catering to diverse skill levels, encouraging experimentation, and providing ongoing support and resources. With these best practices, organizations can effectively prepare their workforce to leverage AI tools, enhancing productivity and innovation in the hybrid workplace.

In hybrid work cultures, balancing AI automation with human interaction and intuition is a nuanced and critical task. AI's role is most beneficial when it complements human capabilities rather than replacing them. This balance is essential for creating a work environment that leverages the strengths of both AI and human employees.

The integration of AI should focus on areas where it can add the most value, typically involving repetitive and time-consuming tasks. By automating these aspects, AI can free human employees to focus on strategic, creative, and interpersonal elements of their work. It's not about replacing human decision-making but enhancing it. AI-driven data analysis, for example, can provide valuable insights, but the final judgments should still harness human experience and intuition.

Creating a collaborative relationship between AI and human workers optimizes efficiency and innovation. AI can manage initial data gathering and analysis, while human employees interpret these findings, applying nuance and context. Training employees in this collaborative approach ensures they understand both the strengths and limitations of AI.

Ethical considerations, particularly the mitigation of biases in AI algorithms, are also crucial. Developing AI systems that are transparent and fair ensures that they support human-centric values like empathy and ethical judgment. Despite the convenience of AI and digital communication tools, opportunities for real-time interactions are essential for maintaining team cohesion and a sense of community. Investing in employee development in areas where human skills are irreplaceable, such as leadership and creativity, ensures that the workforce remains valuable and relevant. Organizations should regularly evaluate the impact of AI on their workforce, making adjustments to ensure that AI automation enhances rather than diminishes the role of human interaction in the workplace.

Maintaining a balance between AI automation and human interaction in a hybrid work environment involves a thoughtful approach. It's about leveraging AI to augment human work, enhancing decision-making, fostering collaboration, and ensuring that the workforce is equipped to work alongside AI effectively. This balance is key to harnessing the full potential of AI in supporting and augmenting the human workforce in hybrid settings.

The integration of AI in hybrid work models brings with it a range of ethical concerns, particularly around privacy and data security. Navigating these concerns requires a thoughtful and strategic approach to ensure the ethical use of AI. One of the primary ethical concerns is the protection of employee privacy. AI systems often require access to large amounts of data, some of which can be personal or sensitive. It's crucial to ensure that this data is collected, stored, and used in a manner that respects employee privacy and complies with relevant data protection laws. This involves implementing robust data governance policies, secure data storage solutions, and clear guidelines on data usage.

Another concern is the transparency and fairness of AI systems. There's a risk of bias in AI algorithms, which can lead to unfair or discriminatory outcomes. To address this, organizations need to prioritize the development of transparent and accountable AI systems. This can be achieved by involving diverse teams in the development and testing of AI systems, conducting regular audits for bias and fairness, and being transparent about how AI systems make decisions. Ensuring data security is also a key ethical concern. With the increased use of AI and cloud-based tools in hybrid work models, safeguarding against data breaches and cyber threats becomes paramount. Organizations should invest in advanced cybersecurity measures, regularly update their systems, and train employees on cybersecurity best practices.

Employee involvement and consent are also important ethical considerations. Employees should be informed about how AI systems are being used in their workplace and the implications for their work. Seeking employee consent, especially in cases where AI tools are used for monitoring or evaluating work, is crucial for maintaining trust. There's a need for ongoing ethical evaluation and adaptation. As AI technology and its applications in the workplace evolve, so should the ethical frameworks that govern its use. Regular reviews and updates of AI policies and practices, considering the latest technological advancements and ethical guidelines, are necessary.

Ensuring the ethical use of AI in a hybrid workplace involves protecting employee privacy, ensuring the transparency and fairness of AI systems, maintaining data security, involving and seeking consent from employees, and ongoing ethical evaluation. By addressing these concerns strategically, organizations can leverage the benefits of AI in their hybrid work models while upholding ethical standards and maintaining employee trust.

It's evident that the thoughtful incorporation of AI technologies can significantly enhance the efficiency, productivity, and adaptability of these modern work environments. This chapter has underscored the potential of AI to transform various aspects of hybrid work, from automating routine tasks to facilitating advanced data analysis and improving communication across distributed teams.

Key insights from this chapter highlight that the successful integration of AI in hybrid workplaces hinges on several critical factors. Firstly, the alignment of AI tools with the specific needs and challenges of hybrid work models is essential. This involves customizing AI applications to enhance flexibility and support both remote and in-office work settings. Secondly, maintaining a balance between AI automation and human interaction is crucial. While AI can optimize efficiency, the unique value of human creativity, intuition, and interpersonal interaction must remain central to work processes.

Addressing ethical considerations such as privacy, data security, and transparency is fundamental to building trust and acceptance among employees. Ensuring ethical use of AI involves implementing robust data governance frameworks, transparent AI algorithms, and involving employees in the conversation around AI integration.

As we transition to the next chapter, the focus shifts to skill development and training in an AI-driven hybrid world. The rapidly evolving landscape of AI in the workplace necessitates a workforce that is not only technologically adept but also skilled in collaborating with AI tools. The upcoming chapter will delve into the strategies and best practices for upskilling and reskilling employees, ensuring they are equipped to thrive in an environment where AI plays an increasingly significant role. We will explore the intersection of AI literacy, continuous learning, and professional development, providing insights into how organizations can cultivate a workforce that is proficient, adaptable, and ready to harness the opportunities presented by AI in hybrid work settings.

# Chapter 10: Skill Development and Training in an AI-Driven Hybrid World

In Chapter 10, we jump into the critical arena of skill development and training in the context of an AI-driven hybrid workplace. This chapter aims to provide an overview of the evolving skill landscape shaped by the integration of AI and the adoption of hybrid work models. It emphasizes the importance of a dual-focused approach to skill development, which caters to both AI literacy and competencies necessary for effective remote working.

The integration of AI into hybrid work environments is rapidly changing the nature of work, leading to the emergence of new job roles and the transformation of existing ones. This evolution brings forth a demand for a unique set of skills that employees must possess to thrive in such a dynamic setting. AI literacy – understanding how AI works, how it can be applied, and the implications of AI decisions – is becoming increasingly important. It's not just about technical skills to operate AI systems but also about understanding the broader context in which these technologies are deployed.

Parallel to AI literacy, there is a growing need for competencies that enable effective remote working. These include digital communication skills, self-management, time management, and the ability to work collaboratively in a virtual environment. In a hybrid setting, where team members may not always share physical space, these skills are crucial for maintaining productivity, collaboration, and team cohesion.

The chapter establishes the need for continuous learning and adaptability. The rapid pace of technological change, especially in AI, necessitates an ongoing approach to learning and skills development. Employees must be equipped not only with the skills needed for today but also with the ability to adapt and learn new skills as work environments and technology continue to evolve.

We will explore the strategies and best practices for cultivating these essential skills in the workforce. This includes identifying key skills for the future of work, designing effective training programs, leveraging technology for skill development, and fostering a culture of continuous learning and adaptability. The chapter aims to provide guidance on how organizations can develop a workforce that is not only proficient in the technical aspects of AI but also adept at navigating the nuances of hybrid work environments.

In an AI-driven hybrid workplace, upskilling the workforce becomes a pivotal aspect of maintaining competitive advantage and operational efficiency. The essential skills required in such environments extend beyond traditional job-specific competencies to include AI literacy and enhanced remote working capabilities.

AI literacy is becoming increasingly important across various job roles and levels, not just those directly involved with technology. Understanding the basics of AI, how it can be applied in one's area of work, and the ethical implications of AI decisions are crucial for all employees. This literacy enables a more informed and engaged workforce capable of leveraging AI tools effectively and contributing to AI-related discussions and decisions within the organization.

The importance of AI literacy transcends technical know-how; it encompasses an understanding of how AI integration impacts workflow, customer interactions, and decision-making processes. Employees at all levels should be comfortable interacting with AI tools, interpreting AI-driven insights, and understanding the limitations of AI technology.

In addition to AI literacy, developing remote working competencies is equally important in a hybrid-AI workplace. This includes skills such as:

- Digital Communication: Effective communication in a remote setting involves more than just sending emails or messages. It requires an understanding of how to communicate clearly and effectively across various digital platforms, adapting one's communication style to different mediums, and ensuring that key messages are conveyed and understood despite the lack of physical cues.

- Self-Management: Remote work often requires a higher degree of self-discipline and motivation. Skills in time management, prioritizing tasks, and setting personal work goals are crucial. Employees should be able to manage their workload effectively without the constant presence of supervisors or the structure of a traditional office environment.

- Virtual Collaboration: The ability to work effectively with a team that is not physically co-located is vital. This includes using collaborative tools, engaging in virtual team meetings productively, and being able to collaborate on projects asynchronously.

Developing these competencies involves a blend of formal training and experiential learning. Formal training programs, whether in-person or online, can provide employees with foundational knowledge and skills. Experiential learning, such as working on cross-functional projects or participating in virtual team-building exercises, can help employees apply these skills in real-world scenarios.

Organizations should also provide resources and tools that facilitate the development of these skills. For instance, access to online courses on AI and digital communication, platforms that enable virtual collaboration, and tools for effective time management can support employees in acquiring and honing these essential skills.

Upskilling for a hybrid-AI workplace involves a focus on both AI literacy and remote working competencies. By identifying and developing these essential skills, organizations can ensure their workforce is equipped to navigate the complexities and leverage the opportunities presented by AI-driven hybrid work environments.

Developing effective training programs for a hybrid-AI workplace involves crafting a curriculum that addresses the unique interplay between advanced technology and flexible work arrangements. These programs should cater to the diverse needs of employees, varying in skill levels and roles, and employ various training methodologies to maximize learning and engagement.

1. Needs Assessment: The first step in creating effective training programs is conducting a thorough needs assessment. This involves identifying the specific skills and knowledge gaps related to AI and hybrid work within the organization. Surveys, interviews, and performance data can provide insights into where training is most needed.

2. Diverse Training Methodologies: Given the varied learning preferences and schedules of employees in a hybrid workplace, it's important to utilize a mix of training methodologies. Online learning platforms offer flexibility and can provide a wide range of courses on AI technology, digital communication, and remote collaboration. Workshops, whether virtual or in-person, can facilitate more interactive and hands-on learning experiences. Experiential learning opportunities, such as project-based learning or simulation exercises, can help employees apply new skills in real-world scenarios.

3. Customizing Training Content: Training content should be customized to meet the diverse needs of different employee groups. For instance, technical teams may require more in-

depth training on AI functionalities and data analysis, while non-technical staff might benefit more from courses on AI applications in their specific work areas and general digital literacy. Leadership training might focus on managing remote teams and integrating AI into strategic planning.

4. Blended Learning Approaches: Combining self-paced online learning with instructor-led sessions can cater to different learning styles and reinforce learning objectives. Blended learning approaches also allow employees to learn the basics at their own pace and then delve deeper into topics through interactive sessions.

5. Continuous Learning and Support: Training should not be a one-time event but part of a continuous learning culture. Regular updates to training programs, refresher courses, and ongoing support such as Q&A sessions, forums, or dedicated helpdesks can assist employees in keeping up with technological advancements and evolving work practices.

6. Measuring Training Effectiveness: Assessing the effectiveness of training programs is essential. This can be done through evaluations, quizzes, practical assessments, and feedback surveys. Monitoring the application of skills in the workplace and the impact on performance can also provide valuable insights into the training program's effectiveness.

7. Promoting a Learning Culture: Encouraging a culture that values ongoing learning and skill development is crucial. This can be fostered by leadership endorsement, recognizing and rewarding learning achievements, and creating platforms for knowledge sharing among employees.

Creating effective training programs for a hybrid-AI workplace requires a strategic and comprehensive approach, employing diverse methodologies, customizing content for varied needs, and fostering an environment of continuous learning and adaptation. By doing so, organizations can ensure their workforce is well-equipped to navigate the evolving landscape of AI-driven hybrid work.

In a hybrid-AI work environment, leadership development takes on new dimensions, requiring a nuanced blend of technical savvy and advanced people management skills. Effective leadership in such settings is characterized by the ability to harness AI for insightful decision-making, manage geographically dispersed teams, drive innovation, and maintain a cohesive team culture.

Training leaders to leverage AI tools for data-driven decision-making is a critical aspect of this development. Leaders need to understand not just the technical workings of AI systems, but also how to interpret and apply the insights these systems provide in making strategic business decisions. This skill is essential for navigating the data-rich landscape of modern business environments.

Managing distributed teams in a hybrid setup is another key area of focus. This requires leaders to master the art of digital communication and develop trust-building strategies that transcend physical boundaries. It's about keeping remote team members engaged, motivated, and connected, despite the lack of face-to-face interactions. Leaders must be adept at recognizing and responding to the unique challenges faced by remote workers.

Fostering a culture of innovation in a hybrid-AI workplace is also vital. Leaders should create an environment where creative thinking and experimentation are encouraged, utilizing AI to uncover new insights and opportunities. Encouraging team members to share ideas freely and embracing a culture of experimentation are fundamental to this process. Ensuring team cohesion in a hybrid environment is a delicate balancing act. Leaders must implement strategies that foster a sense of belonging and team unity, whether through regular virtual team-building exercises, informal online gatherings, or ensuring inclusivity in all team interactions. The goal is to sustain a strong team dynamic, irrespective of where team members are physically located.

Adapting leadership styles to better suit the hybrid-AI environment is also necessary. Leaders may need to shift from traditional command-and-control approaches to more collaborative and facilitative styles. Empowering teams, effective delegation, and providing supportive guidance are key components of this adaptive leadership style. Ethical considerations around AI use are another important aspect of leadership development. Leaders must be cognizant of potential biases in AI systems, the broader implications of AI on employment, and the ethical use of AI in decision-making processes.

Given the ever-evolving nature of AI technologies and hybrid work strategies, a commitment to continuous learning and adaptation is essential for leaders in these environments. Staying abreast of the latest technological advancements and evolving work practices ensures that leaders remain effective and relevant in this dynamic landscape.

Effective leadership in a hybrid-AI context is multifaceted, encompassing technical understanding, people management, innovation, team cohesion, ethical considerations, and a commitment to ongoing learning. By cultivating these diverse skills and qualities, leaders can successfully steer their organizations through the complexities of a hybrid-AI work environment.

In today's rapidly evolving work landscape, especially within hybrid-AI environments, the importance of cultivating a culture of continuous learning is paramount. This culture is crucial for adapting to constant technological advancements and changes in work practices. It's about creating an environment where learning and skill development are not just encouraged but are integral parts of the organizational fabric.

A learning culture in the modern workplace transcends traditional training approaches. It means providing employees with diverse and easily accessible learning resources, including online courses, in-house training sessions, workshops, and educational materials, catering to different learning styles and needs. However, it's not just about making resources available; it's also about fostering a mindset where employees are motivated to take charge of their own learning. This could involve initiatives like offering learning stipends, allocating work time for personal development, and recognizing self-directed learning efforts.

Integrating learning directly into work processes is another key aspect. When training and development opportunities are woven into daily tasks and projects, learning becomes a natural part of the job. For instance, incorporating skill-sharing sessions into team meetings or embedding learning components in project debriefs can reinforce this integration.

Leadership plays a pivotal role in promoting and modeling this culture. When leaders actively engage in their own professional development and openly share their learning experiences, it sets a powerful example for the team. Leaders should not only encourage their teams to pursue learning opportunities but also create an environment that values and supports these endeavors.

Creating learning communities within the organization can also enhance the learning culture. Establishing peer learning groups, mentoring programs, and regular knowledge-sharing meetups can facilitate collaborative learning and knowledge exchange, fostering a sense of community around learning.

Recognizing and rewarding learning and development achievements also acts as a strong motivator. Whether through formal recognition during performance evaluations, learning achievement awards, or casual acknowledgment in meetings, celebrating learning fosters a positive reinforcement loop.

A responsive approach to feedback on learning initiatives is crucial. Regularly gathering and acting on feedback ensures that learning programs and resources remain relevant, effective, and aligned with employee needs and organizational goals.

Building a culture of continuous learning in a hybrid-AI work environment involves more than just providing resources; it's about encouraging self-initiated learning, integrating learning into work, leadership endorsement, fostering learning communities, recognizing achievements, and being adaptable based on feedback. This approach not only prepares employees to keep pace with evolving work demands but also cultivates a workplace that values growth, innovation, and adaptability.

Assessing the impact and effectiveness of training initiatives in a hybrid-AI workplace is a multifaceted process that encompasses various methods and approaches. It's essential to combine both quantitative and qualitative assessments to gain a comprehensive understanding of how well these programs are meeting their objectives. Quantitative measures, such as completion rates and test scores, offer tangible data on learner engagement and comprehension. At the same time, qualitative assessments through participant feedback provide deeper insights into the training's relevance and applicability in the workplace.

Feedback mechanisms play a crucial role in this assessment process. Collecting feedback from participants through post-training surveys, focus groups, or interviews is invaluable in understanding the effectiveness of the training. This feedback should not only be gathered immediately following the program but also after a period during which participants have had the chance to apply what they've learned in their daily work. Such longitudinal feedback helps in assessing the real-world impact of the training.

Observation and monitoring in the workplace are also key to measuring the effectiveness of training programs. Supervisors and managers can observe changes in performance and the application of new skills, offering practical insights into how the training translates into improved work practices.

Conducting a Return on Investment (ROI) analysis is particularly useful for more comprehensive training programs. This analysis looks at the benefits of the training relative to its costs, considering factors like productivity improvements, quality enhancements, and reductions in errors or inefficiencies.

The principle of continuous improvement is central to the success of training initiatives. Training programs should not be static; they need to evolve continuously based on feedback, technological advancements, and changes in job roles. Regular reviews and updates of training materials, methodologies, and content ensure the programs remain relevant and effective.

Assessing the long-term impact of training on career progression and employee retention can offer additional insights. Tracking the career paths of employees who have undergone training can highlight the role of these programs in fostering employee development and satisfaction. Benchmarking against industry standards or peers can provide an external perspective on the effectiveness of training programs. This comparison can help identify areas where the training excels or falls short, offering a benchmark for continuous improvement. Measuring the effectiveness of training in a hybrid-AI work environment is an ongoing process that requires a mix of immediate and long-term evaluation strategies, encompassing both hard data and qualitative feedback. This comprehensive approach ensures that training programs not only meet current needs but are also poised to adapt and evolve with the changing workplace landscape.

In skill development for a hybrid-AI workplace, real-world examples from various organizations provide valuable insights into effective strategies and best practices. These case studies illustrate how different companies have navigated the challenges of upskilling employees in an environment where technological advancements and flexible work arrangements coexist.

One such example is a global technology firm that launched an extensive AI literacy program for all its employees. This initiative included a series of online courses, workshops, and interactive seminars designed to enhance understanding of AI technologies and their applications in various business areas. The program's success was marked by a significant increase in employee engagement and the practical application of AI skills in projects, leading to more innovative solutions and efficient workflows.

Another case study involves a financial services company that focused on developing remote working competencies among its staff. Recognizing the challenges of managing distributed teams, the company implemented a series of virtual training sessions aimed at enhancing digital communication, project management, and collaboration skills. The program also included virtual mentorship and peer-learning groups to facilitate knowledge sharing and foster a supportive learning environment. Post-training assessments indicated improved team collaboration and productivity, with employees reporting greater confidence in navigating the hybrid work model.

A retail organization provides another compelling example. Faced with the need to integrate AI into its customer service operations, the company developed a training program tailored to both technical and non-technical staff. The program covered AI basics, ethical considerations, and customer engagement strategies using AI tools. The training not only equipped employees with necessary skills but also fostered a culture of ethical AI use, enhancing customer satisfaction and trust in the brand.

These case studies reveal several key lessons and best practices. Firstly, the importance of tailoring training programs to the specific needs of the organization and its employees cannot be overstated. Customization ensures relevance and increases the likelihood of successful skill application in the workplace. Secondly, blending various training methodologies, such as online learning with interactive workshops, caters to different learning styles and enhances engagement. Thirdly, ongoing support and opportunities for practical application are crucial for the consolidation of new skills. Finally, involving leadership in the training process, either as participants or sponsors, reinforces the organization's commitment to continuous learning and skill development.

These real-world examples underscore the value of well-designed skill development initiatives in a hybrid-AI workplace. By drawing on these lessons and best practices, organizations can craft more effective training programs that not only build necessary competencies but also support their broader strategic objectives in the evolving landscape of work.

As AI technology continues to evolve, anticipating future trends in skill requirements becomes crucial for maintaining a competitive and effective workforce. Staying ahead in skill development and workforce readiness in the context of an ever-changing technological landscape requires a proactive and forward-thinking approach.

Understanding future trends in AI necessitates a keen eye on technological advancements and their potential impact on various industries. For instance, the increasing use of AI in automation may require a greater emphasis on skills related to AI management and oversight. Similarly, as AI becomes more integrated into decision-making processes, skills in interpreting and making judgments based on AI-generated data will become increasingly valuable.

To prepare for these future skill requirements, organizations can adopt several strategies:

- Continuous Market and Technology Monitoring: Keeping abreast of the latest developments in AI technology and market trends is essential. This can be achieved through regular industry research, attending technology conferences, and fostering connections with tech think tanks and universities.

- Collaboration with Educational Institutions: Partnering with universities and educational institutions can provide access to cutting-edge research and training programs. These partnerships can help in designing curriculums that are aligned with the latest industry needs and technological advancements.

- Employee Skill Assessment and Development Plans: Regularly assessing the skills of the workforce and creating individual development plans can ensure that each employee is working towards acquiring future-relevant skills. Tailored development plans based on both current job requirements and future trends ensure a more targeted and effective approach to skill development.

- Encouraging Cross-Functional Skill Development: In an AI-driven workplace, cross-functional skills become increasingly important. Encouraging employees to develop skills outside their immediate areas of expertise, especially in technology and data analysis, can lead to a more versatile and adaptable workforce.

- Leadership Training: Preparing leaders to manage in a rapidly evolving technological environment is critical. Training in areas such as change management, digital transformation leadership, and AI ethics will equip leaders to effectively guide their teams through technological transitions.

Preparing for future skill requirements in an AI-driven work environment involves continuous learning and adaptability, both at an organizational and individual level. By anticipating future trends, fostering a learning culture, collaborating with educational institutions, and focusing on both current and future skills development, organizations can stay ahead in the dynamic landscape of AI and technology.

It's clear that this aspect is pivotal for organizations navigating the complexities of modern work environments. The integration of AI technologies and the shift towards hybrid work models have created a landscape where continuous learning, adaptability, and technological literacy are more crucial than ever.

The importance of skill development in this context cannot be overstated. As AI continues to reshape the nature of work, employees must be equipped with not only the technical skills to interact with AI systems but also the soft skills necessary to thrive in a hybrid environment. These include the ability to manage remote teams, communicate effectively in a digital setting, and maintain productivity and engagement regardless of physical location.

Key strategies for successful skill development in an AI-driven hybrid world involve a proactive approach to training, focusing on both current and future skill requirements. Organizations must stay ahead of technological trends, continuously assess the skills of their workforce, and provide diverse and accessible training programs. Emphasizing cross-functional and AI-specific skills, fostering a culture of continuous learning, and ensuring leadership is equipped to manage these transitions are all crucial components.

Training should not be seen as a one-time event but as an ongoing process that adapts to the evolving needs of the workforce and the organization. This requires a commitment to continuous improvement, regular feedback mechanisms, and the flexibility to adjust training programs in response to technological advancements and changing market demands.

As we transition to the next chapter, the focus shifts to ethical management at the intersection of AI and hybrid work. This upcoming discussion is critical as it delves into the ethical considerations and challenges that arise when integrating AI into hybrid work models. It will explore how organizations can navigate these challenges, ensuring that AI is used in a way that is ethical, fair, and in alignment with organizational values and societal norms. The intersection of AI and ethics in a hybrid work environment presents a complex but essential area of focus, crucial for building a sustainable, responsible, and forward-thinking workplace.

# Chapter 11: Ethical Management in the Intersection of AI and Hybrid Work

In Chapter 11, we move into the multifaceted and intricate domain of ethical management at the intersection of AI technology and hybrid work environments. This introduction sets the stage for a thorough exploration of the ethical complexities that arise when advanced technological systems are integrated into the modern, flexible work models.

The convergence of AI and hybrid work models brings forth a unique set of ethical challenges and considerations. AI technology, with its capabilities for data processing, automation, and decision-making, offers tremendous benefits for enhancing workplace efficiency and productivity. However, these advancements also raise significant ethical questions. Issues around data privacy, surveillance, algorithmic bias, and the impact of AI on job roles and employee well-being are at the forefront of these concerns.

In a hybrid work environment, where the boundaries between personal and professional spaces are increasingly blurred, the ethical implications of using AI become even more pronounced. The management of data security, the fairness of AI-driven decisions affecting remote workers, and the maintenance of an inclusive work culture are just some of the issues that need careful consideration.

Emphasizing the importance of ethical management in this context is crucial. Ethical management involves not only adhering to legal standards and regulations but also ensuring that the integration of AI in the workplace aligns with broader organizational values and ethical principles. This approach is essential for maintaining trust, integrity, and transparency in the workplace. It fosters a culture where employees feel valued and respected, and where the benefits of AI are balanced with a commitment to ethical responsibility.

As we navigate through this chapter, we will explore various strategies and frameworks for ethical management in the context of AI and hybrid work. We will examine real-world scenarios, discuss best practices, and delve into how organizations can create an ethical framework that supports innovation while safeguarding the interests and well-being of all stakeholders. The goal is to provide a roadmap for navigating the ethical landscape of a technologically advanced and geographically dispersed workforce, ensuring a harmonious balance between technological progress and ethical integrity.

In the current landscape where AI and hybrid work models are increasingly prevalent, building comprehensive ethical frameworks becomes imperative. Such frameworks serve as the backbone for decision-making and operations, ensuring that the integration of AI in hybrid workplaces aligns with core values and ethical standards.

The development of these ethical guidelines is crucial to address specific concerns that arise at the intersection of AI and hybrid work environments. Data privacy, for instance, is a paramount concern, as AI systems often process large amounts of personal and sensitive data. Organizations must ensure that this data is handled responsibly, with strict adherence to privacy laws and a commitment to protecting employee information.

Another significant concern is surveillance. The use of AI for monitoring employee productivity and behavior, especially in remote settings, raises ethical questions regarding employee autonomy and privacy. It's essential to strike a balance where AI aids in workflow management without encroaching on personal boundaries or creating a culture of mistrust.

Equitable treatment of remote and in-office employees is also a critical aspect of ethical AI integration. AI-driven decisions, from performance evaluations to resource allocation, should be fair and unbiased, ensuring that no group of employees is disadvantaged or favored based on their work location.

To create and implement these ethical frameworks within organizations, a multi-step approach can be adopted:

1. Stakeholder Engagement: Involve various stakeholders, including leadership, HR, IT, legal teams, and employees, in the development of the ethical framework. This inclusive approach ensures diverse perspectives are considered, leading to more comprehensive and practical guidelines.

2. Define Core Ethical Principles: Establish clear ethical principles that will guide the use of AI and management of hybrid work models. These principles should reflect the organization's values and address key concerns such as transparency, fairness, privacy, and accountability.

3. Develop Specific Policies and Guidelines: Based on the core principles, develop specific policies and guidelines. These should cover aspects like data handling, AI deployment, employee monitoring, and decision-making processes. Ensure these policies are clear, practical, and aligned with legal standards.

4. Training and Communication: Educate employees and leaders about the ethical frameworks through training programs and communication campaigns. Understanding these guidelines is essential for everyone involved to make informed decisions and act responsibly.

5. Regular Review and Adaptation: Ethical frameworks should not be static. Regularly review and update them to adapt to

new technological developments, legal changes, and evolving workplace dynamics. This process should involve continuous stakeholder feedback and monitoring of AI impacts in the workplace.

6. Implementation and Enforcement: Put mechanisms in place to implement and enforce these ethical guidelines. This could involve integrating ethics into AI system design, establishing oversight committees, and setting up reporting and auditing processes to ensure compliance.

Building ethical frameworks for AI and hybrid work models involves a thoughtful and collaborative approach. It requires defining core ethical principles, developing practical policies, educating stakeholders, and ensuring continuous review and adaptation. By establishing and adhering to these frameworks, organizations can harness the benefits of AI and hybrid work while maintaining ethical integrity and trust.

Navigating data privacy and security presents a complex challenge in hybrid work settings, particularly those influenced by AI. With the increasing reliance on digital tools and data-driven decision-making, safeguarding sensitive information becomes a critical concern. As employees work from various locations, the risk of data breaches and privacy violations escalates, making robust data protection measures essential.

The challenges of data privacy and security in a hybrid-AI environment are multifaceted. AI systems often require access to vast amounts of data, which can include sensitive employee information and proprietary business data. Ensuring the security of this data while it's being used, stored, or transmitted is paramount. Additionally, the potential for AI to inadvertently expose sensitive information or be manipulated for malicious purposes adds another layer of complexity.

Best practices for safeguarding sensitive information in distributed work environments involve a combination of technological solutions, employee training, and policy implementation. Technologically, employing advanced encryption methods, secure cloud storage solutions, and robust access controls are crucial. Regularly updating these systems and conducting security audits can help identify and rectify vulnerabilities.

Employee training is another critical aspect. Workers need to be educated about the importance of data security and best practices for maintaining it, such as recognizing phishing attempts, securing home networks, and safely handling sensitive information. Regular training sessions can keep these practices top of mind.

Legal and regulatory considerations are also integral to data privacy and security strategies. Organizations must stay informed about laws and regulations governing data protection, such as the General Data Protection Regulation (GDPR) in the European Union or the California Consumer Privacy Act (CCPA) in the United States. Compliance with these regulations not only helps in avoiding legal penalties but also builds trust with customers and employees.

Implementing clear data privacy policies is essential. These policies should outline how data is collected, used, stored, and shared, both within the organization and with third parties. They should also detail the rights of employees and customers regarding their data and the procedures for addressing data breaches.

Navigating data privacy and security in a hybrid-AI work setting requires a comprehensive approach that combines technological safeguards, employee education, adherence to legal and regulatory requirements, and clear organizational policies. By prioritizing data privacy and security, organizations can protect sensitive information and maintain the trust of their employees and customers in an increasingly digital and data-driven work environment.

Addressing surveillance and monitoring concerns in a hybrid work environment, especially when AI-driven tools are involved, requires a careful examination of the ethical implications. The use of AI for employee monitoring has grown significantly, offering employers unprecedented capabilities to oversee and analyze worker productivity and behavior. However, this raises serious ethical questions regarding employee privacy and autonomy.

The ethical implications of employee monitoring through AI tools are manifold. On one hand, these tools can provide valuable insights into work patterns and productivity, aiding in resource allocation and performance management. On the other hand, excessive monitoring can lead to a culture of mistrust, potentially infringing on employee privacy and creating a stressful work environment.

Balancing the need for oversight with respect for employee privacy and autonomy is a delicate act. Employers must navigate the fine line between legitimate business interests in monitoring work performance and respecting the personal boundaries of employees. This balance is crucial for maintaining a positive and trusting work environment.

Developing strategies for transparent and ethical monitoring practices involves several key considerations:

- Clear Communication and Policies: Employers should clearly communicate the extent and purpose of monitoring to employees. This communication should include what is being monitored, how the data will be used, and the measures in place to protect employee privacy. Establishing clear policies around monitoring practices ensures that employees are fully informed and can provide informed consent.

- Limiting Monitoring Scope: Monitoring should be limited to what is necessary for legitimate business purposes. Avoiding overly intrusive methods and focusing on performance metrics relevant to job responsibilities is important. Employers should refrain from monitoring personal activities and data unrelated to work tasks.

- Employee Involvement in Policy Development: Involving employees in developing monitoring policies can help ensure that these policies are fair and respectful. Employee feedback can provide valuable insights into what is considered acceptable and effective monitoring.

- Regular Review and Oversight: Regularly reviewing monitoring practices and their impact on employees is essential. This review process can help identify if monitoring practices need to be adjusted to better respect employee privacy and autonomy.

- Legal Compliance: Employers must ensure that all monitoring practices comply with applicable laws and regulations related to employee privacy and data protection. This includes understanding and adhering to regional and national laws that govern workplace surveillance.

Addressing surveillance and monitoring concerns in a hybrid-AI work environment involves striking a balance between the needs of the organization and the rights of employees. By adopting transparent, ethical, and legally compliant monitoring practices, and involving employees in the policy development process, employers can ensure that monitoring serves legitimate business purposes while respecting the privacy and autonomy of their workforce.

Ensuring that AI integration in hybrid models fosters an inclusive and equitable work environment is crucial for maintaining a positive and productive workplace. The use of AI in these settings presents both opportunities and challenges for promoting equity and inclusivity. While AI can streamline processes and provide insights for better decision-making, there is also a risk of perpetuating biases, leading to disparities among employees.

To mitigate biases in AI systems, it's important to first acknowledge that AI algorithms and data sets can reflect existing prejudices, whether related to race, gender, age, or other factors.

Mitigating these biases requires a proactive approach, starting with the diversification of teams involved in AI development. A diverse group of developers and data scientists can provide varied perspectives, helping to identify and address potential biases that might not be evident to a more homogenous team. Also critical is the careful examination and preparation of data sets used to train AI systems. Ensuring that these data sets are representative and free from discriminatory patterns is key to preventing AI from making biased decisions. Regular audits of AI algorithms for biased outcomes and adjustments as needed can also help in ensuring these systems operate fairly.

Beyond technical measures, promoting an inclusive culture in remote and hybrid work setups is vital. This includes initiatives that support diversity and inclusivity, such as diversity training programs, inclusive hiring practices, and policies that ensure all employees, regardless of their location, have equal access to opportunities and resources. Regular virtual team-building activities and inclusive communication practices can help remote employees feel as connected and valued as their in-office counterparts.

Supporting diversity and inclusivity also means providing accommodations and support for employees with different needs. This could involve flexible work arrangements, accessible technology tools, and resources tailored to different learning styles and abilities.

Promoting equity and inclusivity in a hybrid-AI work environment involves a combination of technical diligence in developing and monitoring AI systems and a committed effort to foster an inclusive and supportive culture. By addressing these aspects, organizations can leverage AI to not only enhance efficiency and productivity but also to build a more equitable and inclusive workplace.

In the integration of AI within hybrid workplaces, ethical decision-making becomes a pivotal responsibility for leadership. The decisions made by leaders about how AI is used can significantly impact both the workforce and the broader organization. Navigating these decisions requires a thorough understanding of ethical principles and a commitment to aligning AI use with these principles.

Leadership plays a crucial role in setting the tone for how AI is utilized in the workplace. This involves not just making decisions about which AI technologies to implement, but also considering how these technologies will affect employee privacy, job roles, and the overall work environment. Leaders must weigh the benefits of AI tools against potential ethical risks, such as privacy infringements or biases in AI algorithms.

To assist leaders in this process, several frameworks and tools have been developed to guide ethical decision-making in AI integration. These often involve a set of principles or guidelines that can be applied to evaluate the ethical implications of AI systems. For instance, principles such as transparency, fairness, non-discrimination, and accountability are commonly included in these frameworks. They provide a benchmark against which AI technologies and their applications can be assessed. In addition to ethical frameworks, decision-making tools like ethical impact assessments can be employed. These assessments involve a systematic evaluation of how a particular AI application impacts various stakeholders and whether it aligns with the organization's ethical standards. This process often includes risk assessment, stakeholder consultation, and scenario planning.

Leaders can also leverage advisory boards or ethics committees composed of members from diverse backgrounds and expertise. These bodies can provide valuable insights and recommendations on the ethical use of AI, ensuring that decisions are well-rounded and consider different perspectives.

Training and education in ethics for leaders and decision-makers are crucial. Understanding the ethical dimensions of AI and staying informed about the latest developments in AI ethics can help leaders make more informed decisions.

Ethical decision-making in the integration of AI in hybrid workplaces requires leaders to carefully consider the impacts of these technologies. By using ethical frameworks, impact assessments, advisory bodies, and ongoing education, leaders can ensure that their decisions regarding AI use are responsible, informed, and aligned with both organizational values and broader ethical standards.

Cultivating an organizational culture that prioritizes the responsible and ethical use of AI is essential in today's increasingly AI-driven work environments. This culture hinges on an organization-wide commitment to ethical principles in AI deployment and use, ensuring that AI technologies are leveraged in a way that is beneficial and fair to all stakeholders.

Developing a responsible AI culture begins with clear messaging from the top. Leadership should consistently communicate the importance of ethical AI practices, embedding this philosophy into the organizational values. This approach sets a precedent for decision-making and behavior at all levels of the organization. Training and awareness programs are crucial in educating employees about ethical AI practices. These programs should cover topics like the potential risks and benefits of AI, understanding biases in AI, and the importance of data privacy and security. Training should be designed to be accessible and engaging for employees from various departments, not just those who work directly with AI technologies.

Fostering an environment where ethical considerations are part of everyday conversations about AI is important. This could involve regular discussions, workshops, or seminars that delve into recent developments in AI ethics, case studies, or ethical dilemmas related to AI in the workplace.

Encouraging transparency and openness around AI deployments can also contribute to a responsible AI culture. When employees understand how and why AI systems are being used, they are more likely to trust and engage with these technologies responsibly. This transparency includes being open about the limitations and capabilities of AI systems. Creating channels for employees to voice concerns or suggestions about AI use can help maintain ethical standards. This could be in the form of feedback mechanisms, suggestion boxes, or regular meetings where employees can discuss AI-related topics.

Involving a diverse group of employees in AI-related projects and decisions can also enhance ethical outcomes. Diversity in teams helps to bring multiple perspectives to the table, reducing the risk of unintentional biases and ensuring that AI systems are fair and inclusive. Developing a responsible AI culture is an ongoing process that requires commitment from all levels of the organization. By prioritizing ethical AI practices through clear leadership messaging, comprehensive training, open dialogue, transparency, employee involvement, and feedback mechanisms, organizations can create an environment where AI is used responsibly, ethically, and effectively.

As AI continues to evolve and work models change, preparing for future ethical challenges becomes a vital task for organizations. Anticipating these dilemmas and developing strategies to address them proactively is crucial in maintaining ethical integrity and trust in the workplace.

The future of AI and work models is likely to bring complex ethical issues, particularly as AI systems become more advanced and integral to business operations. These challenges may include increased concerns over privacy as AI becomes more capable of processing vast amounts of data, more sophisticated employee monitoring tools that blur the lines between oversight and privacy invasion, and decision-making algorithms that could inadvertently perpetuate biases.

To stay proactive and adaptable in managing these challenges, organizations need to develop a multi-faceted approach:

1. Continuous Ethical Training and Awareness: Keeping up with the latest developments in AI ethics is essential. Regular training and awareness programs for employees and

leadership ensure that the organization's workforce stays informed about emerging ethical considerations and best practices.

2. Ethical Impact Assessments: Regularly conducting ethical impact assessments of AI systems can help organizations identify potential issues before they become problematic. These assessments should consider the impact of AI on various stakeholders and evaluate whether AI implementations align with the organization's ethical principles.

3. Adaptive Ethical Frameworks: Developing ethical frameworks that are adaptable to change is crucial. As AI technology evolves, so too should the ethical guidelines governing its use. These frameworks should be regularly reviewed and updated to reflect new developments and insights.

4. Inclusive Policy Development: Involving a diverse range of voices in the development of AI policies and ethical guidelines ensures that a wide range of perspectives is considered. This approach can help in identifying potential blind spots and biases in AI implementation and usage.

5. Stakeholder Engagement: Regularly engaging with various stakeholders, including employees, customers, and industry experts, can provide insights into potential ethical challenges and how best to address them. This engagement can take the form of surveys, focus groups, or consultation with external ethics experts.

6. Risk Management Strategies: Developing risk management strategies specific to AI ethics can help in quickly addressing any ethical issues that arise. This involves identifying potential risk areas, monitoring for ethical breaches, and having clear procedures for mitigating any issues.

7.  Leadership Commitment: Strong leadership commitment to ethical AI use is essential. Leaders should model ethical behavior and decision-making, reinforcing the importance of ethics in AI and work practices.

Preparing for future ethical challenges in AI and hybrid work models involves ongoing education, adaptable ethical frameworks, inclusive policy development, proactive stakeholder engagement, specific risk management strategies, and strong leadership commitment. By adopting these strategies, organizations can remain proactive and adaptable, ensuring they are prepared to navigate the ethical complexities of future AI developments and work model changes.

As we conclude our exploration of ethical management in the intersection of AI and hybrid work, it becomes evident that this area is not just an operational necessity but a fundamental aspect of organizational integrity and responsibility. The integration of AI in hybrid work environments presents unique challenges and opportunities, demanding a thoughtful approach to ensure that these powerful technologies are used in ways that are ethical, fair, and beneficial to all.

The critical role of ethical management in this context involves navigating the complexities of AI technology while respecting the nuances of human-centric work environments. It's about balancing efficiency and productivity gains offered by AI with the need for privacy, fairness, and transparency. Organizations must tread carefully to ensure that the benefits of AI are realized without compromising the ethical values and trust that are essential to a healthy work culture.

Developing comprehensive ethical frameworks, addressing surveillance and monitoring concerns, promoting equity and inclusivity, ensuring responsible decision-making, and preparing for future ethical challenges are all facets of this intricate task. The strategies and considerations discussed in this chapter provide a blueprint for organizations to approach AI integration in hybrid work models with an ethical lens.

As we move into the final chapter, the focus shifts to case studies of AI-enhanced hybrid workplaces. These real-world examples will provide valuable insights into how organizations have navigated the ethical complexities of AI and hybrid work. The case studies will showcase practical applications, the challenges faced, and the strategies employed to create ethical, efficient, and productive work environments. These narratives will serve as a guide for organizations looking to harness the potential of AI in their hybrid workplaces while upholding ethical standards and fostering a culture of trust and integrity.

# Chapter 12: Case Studies of AI-Enhanced Hybrid Workplaces

In this chapter, we set the context for exploring real-world examples of AI integration in hybrid work environments. These case studies are crucial in demonstrating how theoretical concepts and strategies around AI and hybrid work models are applied in actual business scenarios. They offer a tangible look at how organizations navigate the challenges and opportunities presented by AI in diverse workplace settings.

As we launch into these case studies, we gain insights into the practical aspects of integrating AI technologies in hybrid workplaces. These examples span various industries and organizational sizes, showcasing the versatility and wide-ranging impact of AI. The case studies highlight not just the technological implementations, but also the human, ethical, and operational dimensions of introducing AI into hybrid work models.

Understanding these real-world applications is vital for comprehending the practical implications of the concepts discussed earlier in the book. They provide valuable lessons on effective AI integration, addressing challenges such as ethical considerations, data privacy, employee engagement, and maintaining organizational culture in a technologically evolving landscape.

The relevance of these case studies lies in their ability to illustrate successful strategies and common pitfalls, offering readers a nuanced understanding of what works and what doesn't in the realm of AI-enhanced hybrid workplaces. As such, they serve as a guide for businesses and leaders looking to navigate the complexities of integrating AI into their work models, providing practical insights and actionable strategies for success.

The chapter on success stories of AI integration profiles a variety of organizations, each with its unique journey of integrating generative AI into their hybrid work models. These stories represent a spectrum of industries, highlighting the versatility and wide-ranging applications of AI in different business contexts.

One such story involves a leading healthcare organization that turned to AI for managing patient data and optimizing treatment plans. Initially faced with the challenge of handling vast amounts of data and ensuring patient privacy, the organization implemented AI systems to automate data analysis and provide predictive insights. The result was not only an improvement in patient care efficiency but also enhanced data security and accuracy.

Another example comes from a retail giant that employed AI to enhance its customer experience and supply chain management. The organization's journey began with the challenge of understanding complex consumer behavior patterns and optimizing inventory. Through the strategic use of AI, it was able to gain deeper insights into customer preferences and streamline its supply chain, leading to increased customer satisfaction and operational efficiency.

In the financial sector, a prominent bank's story highlights AI's role in risk assessment and fraud detection. Initially struggling with the volume of transactions needing verification and the risk of financial fraud, the bank implemented AI algorithms to analyze transaction patterns and identify anomalies. This integration not only enhanced the bank's security measures but also improved its operational efficiency and customer trust.

A technology company's journey in AI integration showcases how it leveraged AI for internal operations, particularly in managing remote teams and project workflows. Faced with the challenge of coordinating a distributed workforce and maintaining productivity, the company utilized AI tools for communication, task allocation, and progress tracking. The outcome was a more cohesive remote work experience and improved project management efficiency.

These case studies collectively showcase a wide range of applications and approaches in integrating AI into hybrid work models. Each story provides insights into the initial challenges faced by the organizations, the strategic decisions made in employing AI, and the outcomes of these integrations. The diversity of industries represented emphasizes the adaptability of AI solutions to various business needs, offering valuable lessons and inspiration for other organizations embarking on their AI integration journey.

The journey of integrating AI into hybrid work environments often comes with its unique set of obstacles. Detailing the specific challenges encountered by organizations during AI integration reveals insights into the adaptive measures and innovative solutions employed to navigate these hurdles successfully.

A common challenge faced by many organizations is the resistance to change, especially from employees who might feel threatened by AI technologies. This resistance often stems from concerns over job security or apprehension about adapting to new ways of working. To address this, organizations have implemented comprehensive communication strategies, ensuring transparency about the purpose and benefits of AI integration. They have also focused on retraining and reskilling programs, reassuring employees about their place in the AI-enhanced workplace.

Another significant obstacle is the technical complexity involved in implementing AI systems. Many organizations initially struggled with integrating AI into their existing IT infrastructure. To overcome this, some sought partnerships with AI technology providers for expert guidance and support, while others invested in upskilling their IT teams to handle AI integration in-house. Collaborative approaches between IT departments, AI vendors, and end-users were crucial in adapting these systems to meet specific organizational needs.

Data privacy and security also posed significant challenges, particularly in industries dealing with sensitive information. Organizations responded by strengthening their cybersecurity frameworks and ensuring compliance with data protection regulations. They employed advanced encryption, regular security audits, and employee training in data privacy to safeguard against potential breaches.

In some cases, organizations faced hurdles in training their workforce to use AI tools effectively. To combat this, they developed tailored training programs, using a blend of online courses, workshops, and hands-on learning experiences. Some also established internal support systems, such as AI helpdesks or peer learning groups, to assist employees in adapting to new technologies.

Maintaining organizational culture and employee engagement in a rapidly evolving AI-driven environment was a challenge. To preserve a sense of community and belonging, organizations adopted strategies like virtual team-building activities, regular check-ins, and platforms that encouraged collaboration and communication.

Overcoming implementation challenges in AI integration involved a combination of strategic communication, technical adaptation, a focus on data security, comprehensive training programs, and efforts to maintain organizational culture. The innovative solutions and adaptive measures adopted by these organizations provide valuable lessons in navigating the complexities of AI integration in hybrid work models.

The integration of AI in hybrid workplaces has led to notable enhancements in productivity and efficiency. These gains are a testament to the power of AI in streamlining processes, automating routine tasks, and providing insights that drive better decision-making. Through specific examples of AI tools and systems used by various organizations, we can see the measurable benefits they have provided.

One notable example comes from a marketing firm that implemented an AI-powered analytics tool. This system was capable of processing vast amounts of consumer data to derive insights into market trends and customer preferences. The result was a more targeted marketing strategy, leading to increased customer engagement and higher conversion rates. The firm reported a measurable increase in campaign effectiveness and a reduction in time spent on data analysis.

In a manufacturing company, the introduction of AI for predictive maintenance transformed their operational efficiency. The AI system analyzed data from machinery to predict potential breakdowns before they occurred, allowing for timely maintenance. This proactive approach led to a significant reduction in downtime and maintenance costs, directly impacting the company's bottom line.

A financial services provider utilized AI-driven algorithms for risk assessment and fraud detection. These systems were capable of analyzing transaction patterns in real-time, identifying anomalies that could indicate fraudulent activity. The implementation of this technology not only enhanced the security of financial transactions but also improved the speed and accuracy of risk assessment, contributing to greater overall operational efficiency.

In HR, an organization employed an AI-powered recruitment tool to streamline its hiring process. The tool used machine learning algorithms to scan resumes, match candidates with job requirements, and identify the most promising applicants. This automation reduced the time and resources spent on the initial screening process, allowing HR professionals to focus on more strategic aspects of recruitment. The organization noted a faster hiring process and an improvement in the quality of candidates shortlisted.

These examples illustrate how AI tools and systems, when thoughtfully integrated into hybrid work models, can lead to significant productivity and efficiency gains. The measurable benefits of AI in these scenarios include increased accuracy and speed in data processing, cost savings, improved risk management, and enhanced operational processes. They highlight the potential of AI to transform various aspects of work in diverse industries, underscoring the importance of AI integration in driving business success in the modern workplace.

The impact of AI on employee experience and engagement in hybrid work settings is multifaceted, influencing everything from work-life balance to job satisfaction and collaboration. As organizations integrate AI into their operations, understanding and managing its effects on the workforce is crucial.

In many cases, employees have reported that AI tools have positively impacted their work-life balance. Automation of repetitive tasks by AI has freed up time, allowing employees to focus on more meaningful and engaging aspects of their work. This shift has often led to reduced stress and a better balance between work and personal life. For instance, an AI-driven scheduling tool used by a consulting firm enabled employees to better manage their time, leading to more flexibility and control over their work hours.

Job satisfaction is another area where AI has had a notable impact. Employees in several organizations have expressed appreciation for how AI tools have streamlined workflows, making their jobs easier and more efficient. AI-driven analytics tools, for example, have provided employees with valuable insights that have enhanced their decision-making capabilities and overall effectiveness in their roles.

The introduction of AI has also presented challenges. In some instances, employees have expressed concerns about the potential for AI to replace human jobs, leading to anxiety and uncertainty. Organizations have addressed these concerns by ensuring transparent communication about the role of AI and emphasizing AI as a tool to assist rather than replace human workers.

Collaboration is another area where AI has had a significant impact. AI-powered collaboration tools have enabled better communication and teamwork, especially important in hybrid work environments where team members might not always be co-located. Feedback from employees in various organizations indicates that these tools have facilitated smoother project management and team interactions, enhancing overall collaboration.

Despite these benefits, it's important to acknowledge and address any negative impacts AI might have on employee experience. Regular feedback channels, such as surveys and focus groups, are vital for organizations to understand their employees' perspectives on AI integration. This feedback can guide adjustments in AI implementation, ensuring that it contributes positively to the employee experience.

AI's impact on employee experience and engagement in hybrid work settings is significant. While it has enhanced work-life balance, job satisfaction, and collaboration for many, it is also essential to continuously monitor and address any challenges or concerns that arise. By doing so, organizations can ensure that AI integration positively contributes to the overall employee experience.

The success stories and challenges of the featured organizations in integrating AI into hybrid workplaces offer a wealth of actionable insights. These experiences culminate in a compilation of best practices that can guide other organizations in their journey towards effectively leveraging AI in similar settings.

A key lesson drawn from these case studies is the importance of aligning AI integration with specific business goals and employee needs. Successful organizations have demonstrated that AI implementation is most effective when it directly addresses identifiable challenges or opportunities within the business. For instance, in cases where AI was used to enhance customer service, a clear link was established between the use of AI tools and improved customer satisfaction metrics.

Another critical insight is the need for thorough planning and gradual implementation. Organizations that excelled in AI integration typically did not rush the process. Instead, they took the time to trial different tools, gather employee feedback, and make iterative improvements. This approach allowed for a smoother transition and greater acceptance of AI within the organization. Employee involvement and training have also emerged as vital best practices. Organizations that actively involved employees in the AI integration process, particularly through training and development programs, saw higher levels of engagement and smoother adoption of AI tools. Employees who understand how AI can assist in their work are more likely to embrace these technologies.

Ensuring transparency and open communication has been another key factor in successful AI integration. Organizations that were transparent about the purpose, capabilities, and limitations of AI technologies fostered a greater sense of trust and collaboration among their workforce. Clear communication about how AI would impact work processes, and addressing any concerns around job security, were crucial in mitigating fears and resistance.

Addressing ethical considerations and ensuring data privacy have been pivotal as well. The best-practicing organizations paid careful attention to the ethical implications of AI, particularly around data use and employee privacy. They implemented robust data governance policies and took steps to ensure that AI applications were free from bias and discrimination.

The importance of ongoing evaluation and flexibility in AI strategies has been a recurring theme. Successful organizations continuously monitored the effectiveness of their AI tools and were open to making adjustments based on changing business needs and technological advancements.

The experiences of these organizations highlight several best practices for integrating AI into hybrid workplaces, including aligning AI with business goals, careful planning and gradual implementation, employee involvement and training, transparency and open communication, ethical considerations and data privacy, and ongoing evaluation and adaptability. These insights provide valuable guidance for any organization looking to harness the benefits of AI in a hybrid work environment.

The long-term sustainability of AI-enhanced hybrid work models is a critical aspect of the integration journey, as showcased in the featured case studies. These organizations not only adapted AI to meet current needs but also considered how these technologies would support their growth and evolution in the future.

A common theme across these case studies is the recognition that AI integration is not a one-time event but an ongoing process. As such, these organizations have developed strategies for continuously updating and improving their AI systems. This approach ensures that their AI solutions remain relevant and effective in the face of changing business landscapes and technological advancements.

Many of these organizations view AI as a key driver for future growth. They plan to expand their AI capabilities by exploring new applications and technologies. For instance, a company that initially implemented AI for customer service analytics is now looking into AI-driven personalization strategies to enhance customer experience further. This kind of expansion demonstrates a commitment to leveraging AI for continuous innovation and improvement. Another aspect of long-term sustainability is the focus on scalable AI solutions. As these organizations grow, their AI systems need to accommodate increasing data volumes, more complex workflows, and a growing user base. Investing in scalable AI infrastructure and flexible platforms has been a priority for these organizations, ensuring that their AI capabilities can grow alongside the business.

Employee skill development in AI is also a key factor in long-term sustainability. Recognizing that AI will play an increasingly significant role in future work processes, these organizations are committed to ongoing training and development programs. This focus on upskilling ensures that their workforce remains adept at using AI tools and can contribute to the organization's evolving AI strategies.

These organizations are mindful of the ethical implications of AI as they plan for the future. They are actively engaged in developing and updating their ethical guidelines and governance structures to ensure that their AI practices remain responsible and aligned with their core values.

The long-term sustainability and growth of AI-enhanced hybrid work models in these organizations hinge on continuous innovation, scalable solutions, ongoing employee development, and a strong ethical foundation. By focusing on these areas, these organizations are well-positioned to capitalize on the benefits of AI now and in the future, ensuring that their AI integration remains sustainable, effective, and aligned with their evolving business goals.

Several key takeaways emerge, painting a picture of the potential future landscape of work environments, and give us a chance to reflect on the journey of integrating generative AI into hybrid models.

A central theme from these case studies is the transformative power of AI in enhancing workplace productivity, efficiency, and decision-making. Organizations across various industries have successfully leveraged AI to streamline processes, uncover insights, and facilitate more effective ways of working. The positive impact on both operational outcomes and employee experiences underscores AI's potential as a crucial tool in modern business landscapes. Another key takeaway is the importance of a thoughtful and strategic approach to AI integration. Successful organizations have shown that careful planning, employee involvement, ethical considerations, and adaptability are essential components of this process. These elements not only ensure a smoother transition to AI-enhanced operations but also foster a culture of innovation and continuous learning.

The case studies also highlight the evolving nature of work models and the growing significance of AI in shaping these models. As AI continues to advance, its role in hybrid workplaces is likely to expand, offering even more sophisticated tools for collaboration, automation, and data analysis. This evolution suggests a future where AI is deeply embedded in the fabric of work, driving both efficiencies and new ways of working.

Reflecting on the journey of integrating generative AI into hybrid work models, it's evident that this is an ongoing process, requiring organizations to stay agile and responsive to technological advancements and changing workplace dynamics. The need for regular evaluation, updates to AI systems, and continuous employee training will remain crucial as AI technologies and applications evolve.

The case studies provide valuable insights into the potential and challenges of AI-enhanced hybrid workplaces. They illustrate a future where AI plays a pivotal role in driving business success and shaping work environments. For organizations embarking on this journey, the lessons learned from these case studies offer guidance and inspiration for navigating the complexities of AI integration, ensuring that their approach is strategic, ethical, and aligned with their long-term goals.

# Chapter 13: Conclusion

As we reach the conclusion of "The Future of Work Now," it's essential to reflect on the journey we've undertaken, exploring the profound transformations in the workplace. This book has navigated the intricate landscape where generative AI intersects with the emerging trend of hybrid work models, illuminating key themes and insights that are shaping the future of work.

From the outset, we inquired into the realm of generative AI, unraveling its definition, evolution, and multifaceted impact on workplace culture. We saw how AI is not just a tool but a transformative force, reshaping job roles, demanding new skills, and challenging us to rethink traditional work practices. The ethical considerations around AI, particularly biases in algorithms and the balance between AI decision-making and human intuition, emerged as crucial themes, underscoring the need for responsible and thoughtful integration of technology in our work lives.

Parallel to the narrative of AI, we explored the rising tide of hybrid work models. This shift, accelerated by global events and technological advancements, has redefined the concept of the workplace. We analyzed how hybrid models blend the flexibility of remote work with the structure of traditional office settings, offering insights into the advantages and challenges of such arrangements. The role of technology in facilitating effective remote collaboration, the nuances of managing remote teams, and the importance of maintaining company culture and employee engagement in a hybrid setting were key focal points.

The journey through these pages has been a chronicle of change, innovation, and adaptation. We've witnessed how the advent of generative AI has intertwined with the shift towards hybrid work models, creating a new dynamic in the professional world. This convergence has brought forth opportunities for enhanced efficiency, creativity, and flexibility, but also challenges that require careful navigation.

Reflecting on these themes, it's evident that the landscape of work has evolved significantly. The fusion of AI and hybrid work models is not just a temporary phenomenon but a glimpse into the future of work—a future that demands agility, continuous learning, and an ethical approach from all of us. As we step forward, the insights gleaned from this book can serve as guiding lights, helping us navigate and shape this ever-evolving landscape.

In "The Future of Work Now," a significant focus has been on the harmonious integration of generative AI into the evolving fabric of hybrid work cultures. This synthesis of technology and flexibility has been a cornerstone of our exploration, revealing transformative effects on the workplace. Revisiting this integration, we see a landscape where AI not only coexists with but actively enhances the hybrid work model, leading to a profound reshaping of job roles, skill requirements, and overall workplace dynamics.

The entry of generative AI into hybrid work environments has been a catalyst for change. Traditional job roles have been redefined, with AI taking over routine tasks and opening avenues for employees to engage in more complex, creative work. This shift has not been without its challenges; it has necessitated a reevaluation of skill sets. The workforce of today and tomorrow needs to be AI-literate, not just in understanding how to work alongside AI but in leveraging its capabilities to enhance productivity and innovation.

The integration of AI in hybrid models has brought a new dimension to remote collaboration. AI-driven tools have bridged gaps, ensuring that communication and collaboration are as effective in remote settings as they are in physical office spaces. These tools have enabled a level of flexibility previously unseen, allowing employees to work in ways that best suit their individual needs while still remaining connected and cohesive as a team.

This integration has also introduced new dynamics in the workplace. Leadership styles have had to adapt to manage teams effectively in a setup that is simultaneously remote and AI-enhanced. The role of managers has evolved from overseeing tasks to facilitating an environment where AI tools are accessible and effectively used by all team members. This evolution has underscored the importance of continuous learning and adaptability, not just for employees but for leaders as well.

The synthesis of generative AI with hybrid work models has been a journey of adaptation, learning, and growth. This integration has reshaped the very essence of how we work, demanding new skills, fostering new ways of collaboration, and encouraging a culture of innovation and flexibility. As we look to the future, this synthesis holds the promise of a more dynamic, efficient, and inclusive workplace, shaped by the combined forces of technological advancement and the human desire for flexibility and connection.

As we contemplate the future trajectory of work, it's clear that the landscape is poised for continued transformation, driven by relentless technological advancements and evolving work practices. In "The Future of Work Now," we have navigated the current state of this landscape, but looking ahead, the horizon is teeming with possibilities and challenges that are likely to shape the global workforce in profound ways.

The integration of AI into the workplace is expected to deepen, with generative AI becoming more sophisticated and ubiquitous. We anticipate a future where AI's role extends beyond task automation to more complex functions like decision-making support, predictive analytics, and even enhancing creative processes. This evolution will likely demand an even higher level of AI literacy across all job sectors, making continuous learning and adaptability essential skills for the workforce.

Hybrid work models, having gained substantial ground, are expected to become a standard practice rather than an exception. The future may see these models becoming more fluid and personalized, with organizations offering even greater flexibility to meet the diverse needs and preferences of their employees. This shift will likely further blur the lines between personal and professional spaces, raising important questions about work-life balance, mental health, and the social aspects of work.

Emerging trends suggest that the future of work will also be characterized by a greater emphasis on employee well-being and mental health. As the distinction between office and home environments becomes increasingly nuanced, organizations might invest more in initiatives that support a healthy work-life balance, recognizing that employee well-being directly impacts productivity and innovation.

Another significant trend is the increasing importance of ethical considerations and sustainable practices in the workplace. As AI becomes more ingrained in work processes, ethical use of technology, data privacy, and fairness will become critical concerns. Similarly, sustainability might emerge as a key factor in work practices and policies, with organizations seeking to balance profitability with social and environmental responsibility.

In the realm of global workforce dynamics, we can expect a continued rise in diversity and cross-cultural collaboration, facilitated by hybrid work models and AI-driven communication tools. This shift will likely bring fresh perspectives and innovation but will also necessitate a deeper understanding and appreciation of cultural differences and inclusive practices.

The future of work appears to be a mosaic of technology, flexibility, and human-centered values. As we move forward, it's crucial for organizations, leaders, and employees to remain agile, open to learning, and ethically grounded. By embracing these principles, the global workforce can navigate the challenges and opportunities of this evolving landscape, harnessing the full potential of AI and hybrid work models to create a more efficient, inclusive, and fulfilling work environment.

As we stand at the threshold of a new era of work, it's important to recognize that the path ahead is lined with both challenges and opportunities. The future work landscape, sculpted by generative

AI and hybrid models, presents a unique set of circumstances that organizations and employees must navigate.

Potential Challenges

Navigating Technological Disruption: One of the primary challenges will be keeping pace with rapid technological changes. Organizations will need to continuously adapt their strategies and operations, while employees will have to engage in lifelong learning to stay relevant in their fields.

Maintaining Human Connection: In a world leaning heavily towards digital interaction, maintaining genuine human connection and workplace culture could become increasingly challenging. Organizations will need to find innovative ways to foster team spirit and a sense of belonging, especially in hybrid or fully remote settings.

Ethical and Privacy Concerns: As AI becomes more integrated into everyday work, issues around data privacy, surveillance, and ethical use of AI will become more prominent. Companies will need to develop robust frameworks to address these concerns.

Inequality and Access: The digital divide could widen, with some employees having limited access to the latest technologies or struggling with the transition to AI-enhanced environments. This divide could lead to inequalities in opportunities and career advancement.

Opportunities for Growth and Innovation

Enhanced Productivity and Efficiency: AI and automation offer unprecedented opportunities for increasing productivity and efficiency. Companies that effectively integrate these technologies can expect to see significant gains in these areas.

Workplace Flexibility and Global Talent Access: Hybrid models offer the chance to tap into a global talent pool, unbound by geographic constraints. This flexibility can lead to a more diverse, skilled, and innovative workforce.

New Job Creation and Roles: AI will also lead to the creation of new job roles and industries, particularly in fields like AI management, ethics, and data security. These emerging fields represent significant opportunities for career growth and development.

Advancements in Employee Well-being: The focus on work-life balance and mental health, accelerated by the shift to hybrid work, presents an opportunity to build more supportive and humane work environments.

While the road ahead is fraught with challenges, it is also ripe with opportunities for those willing to adapt, innovate, and grow. Organizations and employees who embrace this new era with an open mind and a willingness to learn and evolve will be best positioned to thrive in the future of work.

As we navigate the evolving landscape of work shaped by generative AI and hybrid models, the significance of ethical considerations and responsible leadership becomes increasingly pronounced. In the future of work, these factors will be instrumental in steering organizations toward success while upholding integrity and trust.

The integration of AI into the workplace introduces a spectrum of ethical challenges. From issues surrounding data privacy to the potential biases in AI algorithms, ethical management stands as a key pillar in addressing these complexities. It is imperative for organizations to develop comprehensive ethical frameworks that encompass not only the technicalities of AI but also its broader impact on employees, customers, and society.

Transparency and accountability in AI operations and decision-making processes are crucial. Ethical management entails maintaining clarity in how AI systems operate and being accountable for their outcomes. This level of openness is essential in building and sustaining trust among all stakeholders involved.

Leaders in the future workplace must provide clear vision and direction amidst the rapid technological shifts. They need to be visionaries, foreseeing the effects of technological advancements and evolving work models on their organization and industry. Responsible leadership involves fostering an organizational culture that prioritizes and practices ethical values. This means setting an example, promoting open discussions on ethical concerns, and embedding ethical considerations into the organizational decision-making fabric.

Empowering and supporting teams is a critical aspect of leadership, especially in hybrid work environments. Leaders must ensure that all team members, regardless of their work location, have equal growth opportunities and are actively included in collaborative processes. Adaptability is another key trait of responsible leadership, being open to altering strategies and methods in response to emerging ethical challenges and new insights. As we move into the future of work, the importance of ethical management and responsible leadership escalates. These elements are vital for navigating the intricacies of AI and hybrid work environments. They ensure that organizations not only flourish in these changing times but also make positive contributions to the broader societal landscape.

In the dynamically evolving landscape of work, marked by rapid advancements in generative AI and the widespread adoption of hybrid models, the virtues of adaptability and continuous learning stand out as essential for thriving. As we look towards the future, these traits are not just beneficial but necessary for both individuals and organizations aiming to navigate the changing tides of the professional world successfully.

Adaptability, in this context, goes beyond the ability to handle change; it involves a proactive approach to embracing new technologies, work practices, and shifting paradigms in the workplace. For individuals, this means staying open to new ideas, being willing to unlearn and relearn, and being agile in the face of changing job requirements and work environments. For organizations, adaptability is about creating a flexible and responsive culture, one that is quick to adopt new technologies and methodologies and can pivot strategies in response to the evolving needs of the market and workforce.

Continuous learning is the cornerstone of this adaptability. In a world where the half-life of skills is rapidly decreasing, ongoing education and skill development are critical. Individuals must take charge of their learning journeys, seeking out opportunities for professional growth and staying abreast of emerging trends and technologies in their fields. Organizations play a crucial role in facilitating this learning environment. This can be achieved through providing access to training and development programs, encouraging knowledge sharing and collaboration, and fostering a culture where curiosity and innovation are valued and rewarded.

Fostering a mindset of continuous learning and adaptability requires a supportive ecosystem. This includes leadership that champions learning and growth, policies that provide time and resources for skill development, and a work environment that celebrates experimentation and learning from failure. In guiding individuals and organizations in cultivating these qualities, it's essential to emphasize the benefits that extend beyond immediate professional gains. Adaptability and continuous learning contribute to long-term career resilience, personal fulfillment, and organizational sustainability. They are the keys to not just surviving but thriving in the future landscape of work, where change is the only constant.

As we reach the conclusion of "The Future of Work Now," it's important to reflect on the journey we've taken together through the pages of this book. We've explored the vast and intricate landscape of a workplace being reshaped by generative AI and hybrid work models, uncovering the challenges and opportunities that lie within. This exploration has not just been about understanding these changes but also about recognizing the role each one of us plays in shaping the future of work.

Every stakeholder, from business leaders and policymakers to employees and educators, has a critical part to play in this evolving narrative. Leaders and managers are tasked with steering their organizations through uncharted territories, balancing technological advancements with ethical considerations, and fostering cultures that value adaptability and continuous learning. Employees, on the other hand, must embrace a mindset of lifelong learning, remaining agile and open to new ways of working. Educators and trainers are pivotal in equipping the workforce with the necessary skills to navigate this new landscape, while policymakers and regulators must ensure that the transition to these new work models is smooth, fair, and inclusive.

This book's journey concludes with a call to action for all its readers. Embrace the change that is upon us. Be open to the innovations that are reshaping our work environments. Engage with the new tools and technologies, not as passive recipients but as active contributors who can shape their use for the greater good. In this era of rapid transformation, your adaptability, creativity, and ethical considerations will be your greatest assets.

Let us not just witness the unfolding future of work but actively participate in its creation. Let's build a work environment that is not only more efficient and productive but also more inclusive, equitable, and fulfilling for everyone involved. The future of work is not a distant concept — it is happening now, and it is ours to shape.

In the spirit of continuous evolution and growth, we invite you to take the insights from this book and apply them in your professional and personal lives. Innovate, collaborate, and contribute to a workplace that is ready for the challenges of tomorrow. The future of work is an exciting journey, and it is one we embark on together.